A Good Man
IS HARD
TO FIND

A Good Man
IS HARD
TO FIND

ADAM, WHERE ARE YOU?

A Guide to Biblical Manhood
in the 21st Century?

MICHAEL L. HENDERSON, SR.

A Good Man is Hard to Find
by Michael L. Henderson, Sr.

Cover Design by Atinad Designs.

SAINT PAUL PRESS, DALLAS, TEXAS

First Printing, 2014

ISBN-10: 0-9915856-9-0
ISBN-13: 978-0-9915856-9-4

Printed in the U.S.A.

CONTENTS

ACKNOWLEDGEMENTS

Whenever someone accomplishes something that is noteworthy, inevitably there are numerous persons who are either directly or indirectly responsible in some way. I first want to give honor to my Lord and Savior Jesus Christ who transformed my life at the age of fifteen. He is the one who is responsible for my journey into manhood.

I want to thank my wife, Twanna, who has been my biggest supporter. She never stopped believing in me and has been a constant in my life. Thank you, sweetheart!

I want to thank Minister Jason Cummings, PhD, who has been an editing partner on this book and has worked as hard as anyone to make this book happen. Thank you, Jason, for the difference you made! I also want to thank Jason's wife, Dimmis, who supported him while he supported me.

I want to thank the New Beginnings Church family for your prayers, support, and your belief in me as your pastor! You are the best members in all the world!

I want to thank my father who has transitioned from this life. He taught me a work ethic that has served me well. I want to thank my mother who has been a rock to our family for all my life. I also want to thank my family for all your love and support.

I want to acknowledge one of my dearest friends and my covering pastor, John Jenkins, Sr. You have opened many doors and opportunities for me, and I am grateful. Thank you, my friend!

And last but certainly not least, I want to thank and dedicate this book to my son, Michael Jr (MJ). You are my biggest motivation for writing this book. The doctors said that you would not make it, but today at eleven years old, you are stronger than ever. Your life and your strong will has taught me so much about being a real man and being a godly father. You are the joy of my life. I love you, son!

To everyone who has encouraged me along the way to achieve my goals: you are too numerous to name, but please know that you have made an imprint on my life. From my heart to yours, THANK YOU!

INTRODUCTION

"...THEN THE LORD GOD CALLED TO THE MAN, AND SAID TO HIM, WHERE ARE YOU?" (GENESIS 3:9, NASB)

Like the biblical character Adam, we often find ourselves drowning in the poor decisions that we've made. Instead of reaching out to God for help, we make things worse by covering up our mistakes with more mistakes. Adam sinned against God by eating from the very tree that God had warned him was off limits (Genesis 2:16; Genesis 3:6b). Adam made things worse by attempting to cover his moral indiscretion with fig leaves (Genesis 3:7), by running from God's presence (Genesis 3:8) and by shifting the blame of the moral depravity of his family from himself to his wife (Genesis 3:12). It was Adam's biblical responsibility to take the leadership position in the family. God's question was *Adam, where* *are you?* Instead of being responsible and standing up like the man God designed him to be, Adam abdicated his leadership responsibility (Genesis 3:6, 17) and then made matters worse by running and hiding from God's presence at his greatest moment of moral and spiritual need (Genesis 3:8).

Although Adam is a major character of my book, and Genesis provides the backdrop, this is not a book about Adam. This is a book for and about men. It is a prophetic cry to the Adams of this generation to take up their rightful place in their families as leaders of their homes. This is a call for fathers to turn their hearts back to their sons and daughters, and for husbands to become the loving leaders that their wives so desperately desire.

What this book isn't. This book isn't another male bashing book or an opportunity to condemn men. We all have sinned and fallen short of the glory of God (Romans 3:23). Instead, I write this book from the standpoint of a peer speaking to another peer. I don't profess to have it all together. Coming from a household where my father was in the home, but was rarely involved and emotionally disconnected, I have struggled with my own personal journey as a man. In fact, I experienced a great deal of anger and emotional insecurity due to my father's lack of involvement and engagement in my life. There was a boiling internal rage that didn't always come out, but I knew it was always there. I didn't have the understanding of how to address it, or deal with it, so I tried to suppress it, hide it and live with it like a hidden deformity. I attempted to connect myself to other men as role models, who I later found to be struggling with their own identities as men. Searching unsuccessfully for answers, solutions or strategies for my condition, I found none to heal my fractured soul.

For me, an important turning point in my journey as a man occurred in 2003. This is when my wife told me that she was pregnant. It had been seven long years of us trying to get pregnant, and I had peacefully resigned that we would never have children. When she shared the news with me, I was cautiously elated on the outside, and secretly afraid on the inside. For the first time in my life I was forced to reflect on my past, and confront my fear of being a father in ways that I had avoided for years. I never wanted to have children because I was convinced that I would be a failure as a father. I was convinced that I couldn't possibly give my child what they needed, knowing that I did not get what I needed from my own father.

In September of 2003, the Lord blessed my wife, Twanna, and me with a son. Michael Jr. whom we affectionately call MJ, is a special needs child. He is one of the greatest things that have ever happened to me as a man. After his birth, I made a commitment to be there for him and to be intimately involved and emotionally engaged in every aspect of his life. For me, that translated into making a commitment to being there for my son physically and giving him the emotional security I didn't have growing up.

I share my personal life struggle because we all have one. I believe most men will spend their whole lives becoming a good man. We never "arrive." I've spent the last thirty-five years of my life getting a handle on what it means to be a good man, father, husband and member of the community. My life is a testament that this journey called manhood is a marathon and not a sprint. I am committed to continuing to run my race.

There will come times in your journey where you will fall as a man. You have to make a decision that you will get back up no matter what! As a Pastor, husband and father, I've spent the lion's share of my life learning and studying how to be a man God's way. As a trained counselor, I've counseled hundreds of men and couples and have seen the application of biblical principles pertaining to mature manhood and marriage work in my own personal life, and in the lives of persons in my congregation. I am convinced that I have a message from the Lord that will help teach men how to be a good man from a biblical perspective. Like the biblical character King David, God has been gracious and has shown his lovingkindness to me during the lowest moments of my life (Psalm 51:1). I have personally witnessed God transform me from a little boy into a mature man. In turn, I am convinced that I need to spend the rest of my life teaching others how to become the Godly husbands and fathers that God has called them to be (Psalm 51:18).

A Good Man. Being a good man doesn't mean that you are perfect. A good man is a man after God's heart. In other words, he is a man whose heart beats to that of his creator and is willing to live the type of life that pleases God (1 Samuel 13:14; Acts 13:22). Like King David, good men understand that they will make many mistakes in their lives. It is incumbent upon us to reach out to God in those moments and draw from His strength. A good man understands that when he makes mistakes, he cannot cover his mistakes with more mistakes or hide from God. On the contrary, good men understand that although they may *fall* many times in their journey (Proverbs 24:16), when they've made Jesus Christ their Lord and Savior, they will not *fail* (Deuteronomy 31:8; Hebrews 13:5b).

To the men reading this book, whether you are young

or old, married, single, engaged, or pre-engaged…this book was written for YOU. This book is a call for fathers to take their rightful place as mature men in their homes and for father-figures to take their rightful place in the community as mentors to young boys and girls who lack a Godly influence in their lives. Furthermore, while it is the case that not all men are fathers or husbands, all men are sons and have experienced the consequences or benefits of the absence (or presence) of their fathers in their lives. This book will help you understand what being a good husband and father looks like from a biblical perspective, and outline what sons need in their lives so that they can flourish and develop into the men of God that they are called to be.

To The Women in Our Lives. To the women reading this book, this is a tool to help you better understand the men in your life. I want you to understand our challenges and daily pressures as we strive to stay faithful to our wives, rear our children, and work dead-end jobs. We need your help keeping our minds in a place where we aren't drifting away from the things in life that are most important (God, family, purpose/assignment) or lose sight of our ultimate responsibility as the leader, provider and protector of our home. I challenge you to encourage the men in your life to read this book. Men are called to be the leaders of their family and women are called to nurture male leadership. As a nurturer, you can be the biggest encourager to your husbands, fathers, uncles, brothers, cousins, sons, nephews and friends to take their rightful place as leaders in the family. It is so important for us to hear the encouragement, love and support of the women in our lives. We need encouragement that does not attempt to tear us down as men, but rather respects our leadership position in the family. There is nothing like a man who may have failed, who has his daughter, sister or niece come back and tell him that she forgives him. To hear from the women in his life that they appreciate what he has done or even attempted to do as a man, and that they believe God has so much more in store for his life.

Likewise, there is nothing like a wife who decides to encourage her husband with her love and support, instead of condemning him with harsh words, to take his rightful place as the spiritual leader of the family. Find me a wife that lets her husband know that she's committed to following his leadership to the best of her ability, and I will find you a man that is on his way to reaching his full potential. Identifying ways to encourage your husband is crucial. There isn't a man on earth that does *everything* wrong. Identify what he is doing 'right' as a husband and father, then determine to encourage him to continue to develop in those areas and beyond.

I humbly offer this book in order to provide sound biblical solutions to the crisis in male leadership that we are confronted with everyday. We only come to know and fully realize our purpose in life as men through our relationship with God. God is our divine mentor and the source that empowers and aids us to become good men. In this book, I lay out the original plan, purpose and intent that God had for man in the garden, and the extent to which his plan was fulfilled through the life of Jesus Christ. It is my prayer that this book will be a blessing to all men, especially those in the body of Christ. My prayer is that this book will help us get back on track as men so that we are no longer Adams hiding from our God given responsibilities, but instead are mature men who are becoming all that God has destined us to be.

CHAPTER 1 ———————————

A Good Man is Hard to Find

"THEN THE LORD GOD FORMED MAN OF DUST FROM THE GROUND, AND BREATHED INTO HIS NOSTRILS THE BREATH OF LIFE; AND MAN BECAME A LIVING BEING."
Genesis 2:7

Our concept of being a "good man" or "real man" has been   perverted since the biblical character of Adam in the Bible. We often admire male celebrities, athletes, and hip hop artists for their bravado, "tough guy image," or muscular frame and washboard abs. In the United States, we frequently assess manhood and "manliness" using the metric of materialism placing great emphasis on how much money we make, the type of car we drive, or the number of women we've slept with. Jesus Himself warned a Palestinian crowd of listeners: "…Watch out! Be on your guard against all kinds of greed; life does not consist in an abundance of possessions" (Luke 12:15, NIV).

Our concept of manhood places a very low emphasis on more substantive things like our emotional and spiritual life, or our relationship with God. The true indicator of manhood isn't the accumulation of stuff; it is to understand one's God-ordained purpose on this earth and to walk in it. We only come to know and fully realize our purpose in life as men through our relationship with God. More specifically, our journey as men begins when we get in tune with the specific role and function that God has called us to fulfill on this earth. Bishop T. D. Jakes once said: "We must acknowledge that manhood is the call of a lifetime."[1] We never fully become men in the sense of perfection; rather, like the sanctification process, manhood is a lifetime call—a lifetime striving. As we strive to look more and more like Christ, we begin to conform more and more into the masculine image that God originally designed us to reflect. Since the fall of Adam, males have been striving (struggling) to do whatever they can to make it in this world. Before the fall of Adam and Eve, life lived in the Garden was easy. As Adam quickly learned, life outside of the garden was hard (Genesis 3:17-19). Why? It was never God's plan for man to operate and function outside of his perfect provision, protection, and presence.

TRUE BIBLICAL MANHOOD

Although countless movies and plays have been produced on how to find a good man, and numerous self-help books, blogs, and articles have been written on how to be a good man, it is my contention that true manhood can only be understood and realized in the context of God's original plan and design. We can no longer allow society to define us as men. Self-help books, blogs, and articles, or society at large cannot tell us how to become men; only God can do that. Defects in equipment suggest a perversion of its original design. In other words, when an item has a defect, it is incapable of operating according to the intention of its maker. It is only the maker who fully understands the intricacies of the thing that has been created. In these cases, defected cars, cell-phones, or televisions are frequently recalled and sent back to their manufacturer. In like manner, we need to understand that since Adam's fall, we have become like defected equipment. American notions of manhood and masculinity, today, are a perversion of God's original design and intent. Furthermore, we are incapable of either understanding or achieving God's standard and definition of manhood without first going back to the One Who designed us in the first place.

Due to this identity crisis, we don't understand our unique biblical position. Adam was the federal head of all mankind. In other words, it wasn't until after Adam ate the forbidden fruit that sin entered into the world (Genesis 3:6-7; Romans 5:12). Adam was also responsible and called to give account for the spiritual life of his family. Note that although Eve sinned first, God came looking for Adam first, holding him responsible for the indiscretion of the first family.

Created in the very image and likeness of a perfect and Holy God, how did Adam, a man designed from a dusty mold of perfection, find himself in the midst of the Garden, doing the very thing God told him not to do? Adam indulged in the forbidden fruit from the only tree in the Garden that was off limits—the tree of knowledge of good and evil. His eyes were opened, and so also were the eyes of Eve.

While Adam and Eve were distracted trying to find a solution for their newly discovered nakedness, the Creator enters the Garden looking for the man to give account for his actions: "Then the Lord God called to the man, and said to him, *where are you?*" (Genesis 3:9, NASB). This is a frequently misunderstood question. God wasn't asking for Adam's geographical location—as if Adam's hiding place was so good that even God couldn't locate him—rather, He was asking Adam a theological question. Adam, where are you in relation to your divine *purpose*? (Genesis 1:28; Genesis 2:15-16; Genesis 2:19). Why is it that you have irresponsibly neglected your *position* as the head of the family? (Ephesians 5:23) How is it that you find yourself running and hiding from my *presence*? (Genesis 3:8)

After the fall, we find Adam focused on the task of sewing together fig leaves to cover his newly discovered nakedness. Distracted by covering his family's immediate physical need (nakedness), Adam overlooks the more weighty spiritual consequences of his sin. Unlike man, God came looking for Adam to give account. Perhaps equally important, God reveals this scenario for what it really is: a crisis in male leadership.

ADAM AND THE CRISIS OF MALE LEADERSHIP

Adam's sin of rebellion was no light matter. The fact that Adam failed to understand the seriousness of his predicament and the consequences of his rebellion demonstrates a great failure or crisis in his leadership. Adam's "crisis" can best be expressed in the following three ways: First, Adam did not simply fall into sin; he failed to recognize his divine *purpose* and unique *responsibility* to look after all life in the Garden. It was

Adam alone who was initially placed in the Garden and given the unique responsibility to "dress it" and "keep it" (Genesis 2:15). It was Adam alone who received direct command from God not to eat from the tree of knowledge of good and evil (Genesis 2:17). It was Adam alone who was given the special assignment to name every bird and beast of the field (Genesis 2:19-20). In fact, it wasn't until Adam was given an assignment and received God's instructions on how to live (His Word) that Eve comes on the scene (Genesis 2:21-22).

Second, Adam was out of *position*. In the context of the family, God has called men to *lead*, to *provide*, and to *protect*. Adam does none of these according to the third chapter of Genesis (The Fall of Man). He does not lead, choosing instead to follow his wife into sin (Genesis 3:6). He neglected to provide, because he allowed everything that God had given them to be in jeopardy. Adam also fell short as a protector, carelessly allowing the devil to set up camp in his domain (the garden) and establish rapport with his wife.

Finally, instead of running to God at his greatest moment of need, Adam chose to hide from God's *presence*. At the end of the second chapter of Genesis, the author tells us that the first husband and wife were naked and unashamed (Genesis 2:25). Before the fall of man, we can assume the sound of God walking in the Garden brought a sense of peace, comfort, and joy to Adam and Eve. The very fact that Adam and Eve knew what God "sounded like" suggests a level of familiarity. Their nakedness demonstrates transparency, vulnerability, and openness to the Spirit of God. I could imagine that when the earth's first couple heard God, they ran to join Him without hesitation. But this time, after sin entered into the world, when they heard the footsteps or presumably the voice of God entering into the Garden, Adam and Eve were paralyzed with fear and shame, and thus, traded their transparency for suspicion and distance. God's call to (man) Adam, "where are you?", was a rhetorical question that suggests that Adam wasn't where he was supposed to be. Like the Adam of creation, the Adams (Men) of today have a set *purpose* and *position* that can only be fully realized at a set place—God's *presence.*

OUR CRISIS

Lest we make the mistake of judging Adam at his moment of crisis, this generation is confronted with a parallel moment of crisis in male leadership. As promisekeepers.org aptly points out, "Society is crumbling around us. Marriages are collapsing. Pornography is winning the battle for men's minds.

Our children are abandoning the Church." Consider these statistics millenniums after the fall of Adam and Eve:

Compared to children with residential fathers, fatherless children are:

- Twice as likely to drop out of school[2]
- Twice as likely to experience incarceration[3]
- 1.5 times as likely to suffer obesity[4]
- Twice as likely to die at birth[5]
- Four times more likely to grow up in homes below the poverty line[6]
- Twice as likely to be sexually active[7]
- Seven times more likely to become pregnant as a teen[8]
- More likely to experience emotional/behavioral problems[9]
- More likely to use/abuse drugs[10] and commit various crimes[11]

A national crisis: according to the U.S. Census, of the 24 million children in America, today, one out of every three live in homes where their biological fathers are absent.[12] Among Whites, roughly 1 in 4 children reside in homes without their fathers. This is compared to 1 in 3 Hispanic children and nearly 2 out of every 3 African-American children.[13] These patterns are further complicated by other societal trends. Since

1960, the divorce rate has nearly doubled. Today, slightly more than 40% of first marriages end in divorce, down from 50% in 1980.[14]

The number of single mothers has also increased more than fourfold in the last fifty years.[15] During the same period of time (1960 to 2010), White and Black men have experienced incarceration rates more than 2 to 3 times the rate they were exposed to over 50 years ago.[16] These patterns represent a national crisis in male leadership and a breakdown in the traditional American family. As traditional marriages continue to decline, we have increasingly witnessed the rise of a range of new families many of which do not include residential biological fathers. When men are physically present and emotionally engaged in the lives of their families, their wives and children fare much better. Consider these findings:

When husbands and fathers are present physically and involved/engaged in the lives of their families:

- Marital happiness/satisfaction is significantly higher[17]
- The odds of a marriage ending in divorce or separation decreases significantly[18]
- Wives experience relatively problem-free pregnancies and good postpartum mental health[19]

For children, father-child contact is associated with:

- Higher scores on reading achievement, mathematics and better overall grades[20, 21, 22]
- Higher IQs and fewer behavioral problems[23]
- Greater moral maturity and better decision-making skills[24]

For adult children, father-child contact early in life is associated with:

- Higher life satisfaction, self-esteem and mental health outcomes [25, 26, 27]
- Greater involvement and positive engagement in the lives of their own spouses and children[28]
- More secure and healthy relationships and greater success in their careers later in life [29]

Here's my point: Men matter, and they play a central role in the lives of their wives and children.

THE BIG SHIFT: CHANGING OUR MINDSET

Change never occurs until we first begin to change the way we think. Since Adam, our sense of masculinity or maleness has been distorted and we are in desperate need of a paradigm shift. Like Adam, our definition of manhood overwhelmingly revolves around the fulfillment of our material and physical needs. We've traded in the embroidery of fig leaves for equally temporal and shortsighted goals like fame, fortune, and success. As Keith Hunt points out in *Acts* Magazine:

> Millions of men live in search of fame, fortune, and success. They think that if they could just make more money or get a promotion, everything would be better. Their emphasis is on the temporal. They live to glorify themselves. But all of this is in vain. Like the sands of time, temporal things eventually fade away.[30]

It is my prayer that this book will be a blessing to the body of Christ. My desire is that my fellow brothers get back on track as men so that we can collectively step up to our God-given responsibilities and become all that God has destined us to be. God is calling out to the Adams of this generation: Adam, where are you? It is my hope that by the end of this book you will only answer in the affirmative: Here I am, Lord, *positioned* where You've called me to be. Here I am, Lord, ready to fulfill my *purpose*. Here I am, Lord, running to be in Your *presence*. I am Adam. You are Adam. Adam, it is now OUR time. It's time to show up. It's time to stand up. It's time to stand out.

Footnotes

1 Jakes, T.D. *He-Motions: Even Strong Men Struggle.* New York: Berkley Publishing Group. 2004.

2 U.S. Department of Health and Human Services. National Center for Health Statistics. *Survey on Child Health.* Washington: GPO, 1993

3 Harper, Cynthia C. and Sara S. McLanahan. "Father Absence and Youth Incarceration." *Journal of Research on Adolescence.* 14 (September 2004): 369-397.

4 Keane, Eimear, Richard Layte, Janas Harrington, Patricia M. Kearney and Ivan J. Perry. "Measured Parental Weight Status and Familial Socio-Economic Status Correlates with Childhood Overweight and Obesity at Age 9." PLOS ONE 7.8 (2012): 1-9.

5 Matthews, T.J., Sally C. Curtin, and Marian F. MacDorman. Infant Mortality Statistics from the 1998 Period Linked Birth/Infant Death Data Set. *National Vital Statistics Reports*, Vol. 48, No. 12. Hyattsville, MD: National Center for Health Statistics, 2000.

6 U.S. Census Bureau, *Children's Living Arrangements and Characteristics: March 2011*, Table C8. Washington D.C. 2011.

7 Ellis, Bruce J., John E. Bates, Kenneth A. Dodge, David M. Ferguson, L. John Horwood, Gregory S. Pettit, and Lianne Woodward. "Does Father Absence Place Daughters at Special Risk for Early Sexual Activity and Teenage Pregnancy." *Child Development* 74 (May/June 2003): 801-821.

8 See footnote 7

9 Osborne, C., & McLanahan, S. (2007). Partnership instability and child well-being. *Journal of Marriage and Family*, 69, 1065-1083.

10 Hoffmann, John P. "The Community Context of Family Structure and Adolescent Drug Use." *Journal of Marriage and Family*, 64 (May 2002): 314-330.

28

11 Bush, Connee, Ronald L. Mullis, and Ann K. Mullis. "Differences in Empathy Between Offender and Nonoffender Youth." *Journal of Youth and Adolescence* 29 (August 2000): 467-478

12 Kreider, Rose M. and Renee Ellis, "Living Arrangements of Children: 2009," Current Population Reports, p. 70-126, U.S. Census Bureau, Table 1. Washington, DC. 2011.

13 See footnote 12

14 Wilcox, W. Bradford. "The Evolution of Divorce." *National Affairs.* (Fall 2009): 81-94.

15 Pew Research Center. "The Rise of Single Fathers: A Nine-fold Increase since 1960." (July 2, 2013). p. 1-8.

16 Pew Research Center. "King's Dream Remains an Elusive Goal; Many Americans See Racial Disparities." (August 22, 2013). p. 1-42.

17 Galovan, Adam M., Erin Kramer Holmes, David G. Schramm and Thomas R. Lee. "Father Involvement, Father-Child Relationship Quality, and Satisfaction with Family Work: Actor and Partner Influences on Marital Quality." *Journal of Family Issues.* (2013): 1-22.

18 Gottman, John M. and Robert W. Levenson. "The Timing of Divorce: Predicting When a Couple Will Divorce Over a 14-Year Period." (2000). *Journal of Marriage and Family.* 62: 737-745.

19 Gjerdingen, D.K, D. Froberg and P. Fontaine. "The Effects of Social Support on Women's health during pregnancy, labor, delivery, and postpartum period." (1991): *Family Medicine.* 23: 370-375.

20 Howard ,K.S., Burke Lefever, J.E., Borkowski, J.G. & Whitman, T.L. (2006). Fathers' influence in the lives of children with adolescent mothers. *Journal of Family Psychology*, 20(3): 468-476.

21 Radin, N. & Russell, G. (1983). Increased father participation and child development outcomes. *Fatherhood and Family Policy*, eds. M.E. Lamb and A. Sagi, Lawrence Erlbaum: Hillside, N.J.

22 Nord, Christine Winquist, and Jerry West. Fathers' and Mothers' Involvement in Their Children's Schools by Family Type and Resident Status. (NCES 2001-032). Washington, D.C.: U.S. Department of Education, National Center for Education Statistics, 2001.

23 Yogman, M. W. Kindlon, D., & Earls, F. (1995). Father involvement and cognitive/behavioral outcomes of preterm infants. *Journal of the American Academy of Child and Adolescent Psychiatry,* 34, 58-66.

24 Mosley, J., & Thompson, E. (1995). Fathering Behavior and Child Outcomes: The role of race and poverty. In W. Marsiglio, (Ed.), *Fatherhood: Contemporary theory, research, and social policy* (pp. 148-165). Thousand Oaks, CA: Sage, 1995.

25 Pleck, J.H., & Masciadrelli, B.P. (2004). Paternal involvement by U.S. residential fathers: Levels, sources and consequences. In M.E. Lamb (Ed.) *The Role of the Father in Child Development,* 4th Edition (pp.222-271), Hoboken, N.J.: Wiley.

26 Sarkadi, A., Kristiansson, R., Oberklaid, F. & Bremberg, S. (2008). Fathers' involvement and children's developmental outcomes: A systematic review of longitudinal studies. *Acta Paediatrica,* 97, 153-158.

27 Peters, B., & Ehrenberg, M.F. (2008). The influence of parental separation and divorce on father-child relationships. *Journal of Divorce and Remarriage,* 49, 78-109.

28 See note 25

29 Grossmann, K. E., Grossman, K., Winter, M., & Zimmerman, P. (2002). Attachment relationships and appraisal of partnership: From early experience of sensitive support to later relationship representation. In L. Pulkkinen & A. Caspi (Eds.), *Paths to successful development: Personality in the life course.* pgs. 73-105. New York: Cambridge University Press.

30 Hunt, Keith. "Crisis of Male Leadership: The Beginning of Real Manhood." *Acts* Magazine. November 2006. Print.

30

CHAPTER 2 ——————

Adam and Eve: The Rock Stars of Creation

From the very beginning, God had something special in mind when He created Adam and Eve. We can think of the Word of God in general, and the first several chapters of Genesis in particular, as a blueprint for God's original plan and design for how men and women were to function and relate to one another on the earth. Mature manhood (or womanhood for that matter) cannot be properly defined outside of God's original plan and intention for mankind and male-female relations in the Garden.

It is important to first establish that Adam and Eve were unique and distinct from all other creation. God spent the first five days of creation and presumably the earlier portion of the sixth day speaking things into existence. We learned that on the first day of creation, God said, "let there be light," and there was light (Genesis 1:3). On the second day, we learned that God said, 'let there be an expanse in the midst of the waters,' and it was so (Genesis 1:6-8). On the third day, God said, 'let the waters be gathered together in one place and let the earth sprout forth vegetation,' and nature was forced to obey His Word (Genesis 1:9-13). On the fourth and fifth day, God said, 'let there be lights in the heavens (Genesis 1:14), living creatures in the sea and birds in the sky,' and it was so (Genesis 1:20-23). During the beginning of the sixth day, God said, 'let the earth bring forth every animal that walks on the earth' (Genesis 1:24-25). Near the latter half of the sixth day, however, God does something different. He pauses and says, "let us make man (or mankind) in our image, according to our likeness" (Genesis 1:26).

No other living creature or object in the sea, in the sky or on the face of the earth boasted such a distinction. In fact, although God spoke things into existence for five and a half days, by the end of the sixth day, the Bible doesn't say that He spoke mankind into existence. It says that *he formed* Adam from the dust of the earth (Genesis 2:7). Let's pause here a moment. We cannot overlook the relevance of this central turning point of creation. The word "to form" (*yatsar*) in the Hebrew can be transliterated to mean to form, frame, or fashion something in the same manner that a potter would design pottery using lumps of clay. There is something special and intimate when an artist forms or designs something with his or her hands. The word form here suggests that when God created Adam, He intended to initiate a unique and intimate relationship with him that differed from all other creation.

God also did something perhaps even more astounding. He breathed into Adam's nostrils the breath of life; and man became a living soul. The mere fact that God formed man in His image and likeness and breathed in his nostrils the breathe of life, signifies the extent to which God valued mankind in both their position and worth. When God breathed into man's nostrils the breathe of life, He deposited something special into man (His essence) and left a part of Himself in man that uniquely set man apart from every animal and object created. Eve also enjoyed this special distinction, with God fashioning the rib (flesh and bone) of the man into her. Although the details of Adam and Eve's creation differ, we are assured in Genesis 1:27 that: "God created man (or mankind) in his own image, in the image of God He created [them]; male and female (NASB)." In other words, both Adam and Eve were created as bearers of God's image and likeness. Created in the image of God, they were built to look like God, to talk like God, and to walk like God. After each day of creation, God looked at His handiwork and said that it was good. But after God created Adam and Eve, He said it was VERY good (Genesis 1:28). For the first six and a half days of creation, God created the backdrop and supporting cast members of the creation narrative. But by the end of the sixth day, God declared that His work was "very good," it was complete, and it was worthy of rest (Genesis 2:2). Adam and Eve were no doubt the main characters and rock stars of creation. They alone enjoyed the unique distinction of bearing God's image.

One way for us to understand the concept of Adam and Eve being created in the image of God is to consider that God has both feminine and masculine attributes that are reflected throughout Scripture. The prophet Isaiah, for instance, describes God's relationship with Israel as a "mother who comforts her child" (Isaiah 66:13, NIV). In Psalm 103:8, the Lord is described as compassionate, gracious, and abounding in love. Furthermore, at least twenty-three times in the Old Testament, the Lord is referred to as El Shaddai. El Shaddai is the plural Hebrew word for the one who has breasts or the double breasted one. This suggests that God nourishes, sustains, and strengthens like a breast-feeding mother would a newborn child.

On the other hand, God is also expressed in a masculine way throughout Scripture. Perhaps most obvious is that God is referred to as "our Father" nearly thirteen times in the Old Testament and Jesus spoke of God being "our Father" nearly thirty times in the New Testament. In Isaiah 62:5, God is referred to as a bridegroom and the children of Israel His bride. Finally, in Psalm 24:8, God is referred to as a mighty King who is strong in battle. This is not a claim that God is both male and female, but rather that God has both feminine and masculine attributes. Given that both Adam and Eve were created in God's image and these were perfect beings, this suggests that God is fully or perfectly imaged or reflected in the pairing of a Godly man and woman. Throughout Scripture, we see this principle realized. This is not an accident, but rather, a biblical reality and principle from creation.

GOD'S DIVINE ORDER FOR ADAM AND EVE: EQUAL IN VALUE

It is erroneous biblical doctrine to suggest that women, in general, and Eve, in particular, were designed lesser in value or worth than Adam. Beliefs of that nature reflect misguided cultural perspectives or a complete misreading of Scripture relating to the personhood of males and females altogether. On the contrary, Adam and Eve were designed as spiritual equals, that is, being equal in person and value. The first chapter in Genesis clearly highlights this point.

First, Adam and Eve were both created in the image and likeness of God (Genesis 1:27). The Bible doesn't say anywhere that Eve was an "incomplete" or "inferior" reproduction of God's image. Instead, we clearly read in Genesis 1:27 that God created mankind in His own image and likeness, both male and female (see also Genesis 5:2).

Second, Adam and Eve were equally blessed by God, and were simultaneously commanded to be fruitful and multiply (Genesis 1:28). In other words, Eve did not receive a lesser blessing than Adam, and as a couple, they were commanded to accomplish that which they could not do separately (be fruitful and multiply).

Finally, both Adam and Eve were commanded to subdue and rule over the fish of the sea, the birds in the sky, and every living thing that moves on the earth (Genesis 1:28-29). In other words, the first husband and wife were called to function as co-rulers and have collective dominion over all life in the Garden. The fact that Adam and Eve were equal bearers of God's image, were equally blessed, and were commanded to co-rule, highlights that God valued Adam and Eve equally. In this way, Eve was

Adam's perfect companion and spiritual equal.

GOD'S DIVINE ORDER FOR ADAM AND EVE: DISTINCT IN POSITION

While the first chapter of Genesis clearly establishes that Eve was Adam's spiritual equal, created in the image of God, equally blessed and called to co-rule alongside her husband, the second and third chapters of Genesis add additional complexity to the creation narrative. Although Adam and Eve were spiritual equals—partners in the sense of their worth, value, and co-rulership—they differed in their position in the context of the family. That is, God expected Adam to take a unique leadership role and gave him a distinct burden of responsibility that placed the care of the Garden and the welfare of his family on his shoulders.

Consider for instance that immediately after Adam was created, the Bible says that God planted a garden toward the east of Eden; and took the man and placed him in it to "cultivate it" and "keep it" (Genesis 2:8; 15). Notice that while Adam and Eve both were to operate as co-rulers, Adam was given the unique responsibility to run and manage the Garden. The Hebrew word for "cultivate" is *abad*, which means to work, labor, till, and to serve unto God in a Levitical or priestly sense. Likewise, the Hebrew word for "to keep," *shamar*, can be interpreted to mean to guard, have charge of, protect and watch over. Together these words demonstrate that God gave Adam the divine assignment to protect and watch over the Garden and that this work and service unto God was so weighty that it was priestly or Levitical in nature. I want to be clear that Adam and Eve did not equally share the burden of responsibility of caring for the Garden and all the inhabitants in it; this responsibility fell squarely on the shoulders of Adam. Eve was yet to be created and there is no biblical evidence to suggest that she was also given this responsibility.

After being placed in the Garden, Adam was also given clear instructions that he could eat freely from any tree in the Garden except the tree of the knowledge of good and evil (Genesis 2:16-17). Again, this occurred before Eve came on the scene, and there is no biblical evidence to suggest that Eve also heard this command from God on a first hand basis. In this way, not only was it Adam's divine assignment and responsibility to run and watch over the Garden, it was also his responsibility to be a guardian of God's commandment, or in the context of his roles and responsibility as a future husband and father, a guardian of the spiritual welfare of the family. This is why although Eve sinned first (Genesis 3:6), God came looking for Adam first to give account or answer for the moral rebellion of the family (Genesis 3:9).

Adam did not simply fall into sin; he failed to recognize his divine *purpose* and unique responsibility to look after all life in the Garden.

As we will see, in the context of the family, God has called men to *lead, provide,* and *protect.* Adam does none of these things in the third chapter of Genesis (The Fall of Man). He does not lead (Genesis 3:6). He neglected to provide (Genesis 3:24) and fell short as a protector (Genesis 3:1-7).

It's difficult and, perhaps, impossible to define manhood in the context of the family outside of how men relate to the women and children in their lives and how they deal with the world around them. It is in this vein, that I use the next chapter to provide a working definition for mature manhood or masculinity in the context of the family that provides the basis for the remainder of this book.

CHAPTER 3 ———————

Manhood: God's Original Plan

What does it mean to be a man, and how can we best describe what being a good man looks like? Having come from a household where my father was in the home but we weren't close, I've spent the lion's share of my life struggling with my own identity as a man. In fact, the one meaningful conversation I had with my father about manhood occurred when I was eleven years old. He sat me down to tell me about the birds and the bees. Our conversation lasted about five seconds. My dad sat me down, looked me up and down and said: "Boy … don't bring any babies home." At the time, I was too young to even comprehend what he meant. Confused, his advice, while well-meaning, raised more questions than answers.

Over the years, the angst that I felt only increased. Although I saw my father every day of my young adult life, I recall having very few significant moments with him and spent most of the time having virtually no conversations at all. It is an understatement to say that I felt lost and abandoned. I was forced to navigate and figure out on my own what being a man looked like. All I could do is take the unspoken messages (whether good or bad) that I learned from my dad as I observed him growing up. On one hand, I watched my dad work everyday and provide for the financial needs of my family. On the other hand, I watched him drink and party with his friends and send the family to church while he stayed at home. Left with a distorted view of masculinity, I was convinced that men worked hard, partied hard, and slept with as many women as they could get their hands on.

My sense of masculinity was clearly distorted. It's probably not surprising that my first marriage failed horribly. I married when I was twenty-one years old. Although I was an adult chronologically, I was a boy masquerading as a man. At the time, I was still trying to figure out who I was. I reached out to other men, but struggled to get what I needed. Not only was my view of masculinity distorted, I had no clue what it meant, or what it took, to be a good husband. My understanding of "manhood" came from observing my father. When conflict arose in my marriage, the only thing I knew to do was to work and be the best provider I could be. I was convinced that if I worked hard, the problems in my marriage would go away— that everything would magically work itself out. I didn't know what else to do as it seemed to work for my father. I had no other models to draw from.

When my marriage began to deteriorate, and providing for my wife didn't solve the problems in my marriage, I hid, and went into an internal shell. To further complicate matters, I was a young minister and pastor of a church. I studied the Bible for answers, fasted and prayed, helped other people with their problems, but had no answers for my own. I did not have the capacity or know-how to properly communicate or connect emotionally with my spouse. I didn't know how to reach out to my wife, how to be vulnerable, how to be expressive with my feelings, or how to demonstrate my love effectively through my words and actions.

The marriage ended in a divorce. I was left to pick up the pieces. I felt hopeless. I felt like a failure. I was a broken man, and felt like a disgraced pastor. I later left my ministry. I was convinced that the Lord could never use me again. I was convinced that there was no hope for me and that I could never be restored. I've since learned what a biblically mature man looks like and have been able to model it in my personal life. I experienced God's forgiveness, love, and restoration.

Today, I consider myself to be a very blessed man. I met and married a wonderful, supportive, and loving woman. My wife, Twanna, and I have shared nearly twenty wonderful years together. They have truly been the best years of my life! As a family, we have activated our faith and have watched God do some awesome things in our personal and spiritual lives. We started New Beginnings Church in October 1999, in a recreational center in Charlotte, NC, with ten members. In only ten years, we transitioned to four Sunday services, grew to nearly 5,000 members, and were blessed to build a 30,000 square foot, multipurpose family life center. My wife and I have been been blessed over the past fifteen years to serve, preach, teach, and encourage others in ministry side-by-side. We continue to build, and our membership has now grown to 7,000. My life is a testament that despite the failures and mistakes you may have made (and probably will make) as a man, there is always hope!

I am sure that I am not alone in my experience and especially in my failures. Few men have the testimony that they received sound and clear guidance on what a good or Godly man looks like that reinforced their young adulthood in positive ways. I believe that my father did the best that he knew how. He wasn't close to his own father. My grandfather was a pastor, but he was so busy and emotionally unavailable that he lost his son as he modeled what he felt was good fatherhood. I believe that many of us do the best that we know how. When our knowledge is limited, however, and we don't know any better, it generally means that we need to know more, so that we can do better.

MISSING THE MARK: DEFINING MANHOOD BY THE WORLD'S STANDARD

We get little help from the Merriam Webster dictionary, which defines manhood as "the state or period of being a man rather than a child." A circular definition, manhood in general, and being a man in particular, has to be more than simply not being a child. If this were the case, all adult males would qualify as men; yet, true manhood has little to do with an individual's age. Society says that when boys turn eighteen they are no longer children or dependents of their parents. From a legal standpoint, turning eighteen also grants certain rights and privileges including the right to vote or join the armed forces. Despite such recognition and benefits, however, eighteen-year-old boys often struggle with their identities and struggle in their self-conceptualization as men. Other age milestones like turning twenty-one, thirty, forty, or fifty do not demarcate the transition from boyhood to manhood either. As a trained counselor and pastor with over thirty years of experience, I've encountered countless males who go through life struggling with their manhood. Some men spend a lifetime questioning whether or not they have ever become men.

Adding to the confusion, our definitions of manhood are seldom based on the Word of God. In the United States, being a good man is often viewed through the lens of materialism. Our social and cultural metric for masculinity or machismo is based on how much money we make, the type of car we drive, how much we can bench press, or the number of women we've slept with. Here is the problem with societal definitions of manhood: they are imperfect, imprecise, and frequently change from one generation to the next. Today, we live in a generation where manhood is rarely modeled, male mentorship is scarce, and a growing percentage of American children live in households without their father. If we are to fully understand what it means to be a man, we cannot go to society or the media to get our answers; we must go back to God's original plan and design as expressed in the first several chapters of Genesis.

As men, we are created and designed by God. It is God, and God alone, Who fully understands our intricate make-up as men, and it is God alone Who can show us how to function with the greatest amount of success in our lives.

BULL'S EYE: GOD'S PERSPECTIVE MATURE MEN, FATHERS, AND HUSBANDS

Mature manhood or masculinity can be summed up with one word: responsibility. The word *responsibility* is a compound term, which includes two words: "response" and "ability." In other words, responsibility in the biblical sense, is our response to the ability or capacity that God has given us as men. When God created Adam, He gave him a specific assignment to guard and care for the Garden and all life in the Garden (Genesis 2:15,19-20), explicit instructions/boundaries not to eat from the tree of the knowledge of good and evil (Genesis 2:16-17), and designated authority to rule or walk in dominion (Genesis 1:26, 28). Biblically mature men understand their divine assignment and purpose on this earth; they have a strong conviction to obey the instructions and boundaries that God has given them, and they recognize and walk in their God given authority. In other words, God's men understand who they are, whose they are, and what they have. When they understand this, mature men properly respond to and fully operate in their God-given ability and authority. Immature men, on the other hand, run from or neglect their God-given ability and authority, thus failing to become all God has called them to be.

In the book, *Recovering Biblical Manhood and Womanhood: A Response to Evangelical Feminism*, John Piper argues that mature manhood or masculinity can best be described as a "sense of benevolent responsibility to lead, provide for and protect women in ways appropriate to man's differing relationships" (p. 35).[1] From this definition, I would like to extrapolate my own, which characterizes what I believe reflects how we can best describe what a mature husband and father looks like in a biblical sense. Mature husbands and fathers are men who understand and embrace their biblical responsibility to function as loving and compassionate leaders of their homes, and who provide for and protect their wives and children in ways that reflect their differing relationships.[2]

Similar to John Piper's definition, I recognize that a husband or father can be mature in his masculinity if he "understands" and "embraces" his biblical responsibility to his wife and children, even if his circumstances restrict his ability to provide for or protect his family. By circumstances, I am referring to situations that are generally out of one's control.

Some men experience chronic or temporary periods of unemployment despite genuine attempts to secure a job and provide for their families. Other men are overseas or in the armed forces and struggle to fully protect their families due to distance. Health issues may also complicate one's ability to provide for or protect one's family. Men who are paralyzed or have debilitating diseases may find it difficult to support their families financially or to physically protect their wives and children. Men in these special circumstances are still considered mature husbands and/or fathers if they understand and embrace their biblical responsibility as leaders, providers and protectors of their wives and children, and would properly fulfill their responsibility if circumstances were different.

THE BOTTOM LINE

So what's the bottom line? What's the point of all this? I'm sure many who are reading this book are probably saying to themselves, "Of course it is the responsibility of husbands and fathers to lead, provide for, and protect their wives and families—everyone knows that." Yet in all of our knowledge or lack thereof, the divorce rate, the number of unhappily married couples and the large share of fatherless homes in the U.S. demonstrates that we are failing horribly. Understanding the threefold responsibility of husbands and fathers to lead, provide for, and protect their families isn't a difficult task. What is much more difficult, however, is understanding how mature husbanding and fatherhood should be modeled.

I believe that we cannot properly fulfill our responsibilities as husbands and fathers to lead, provide, and protect unless we are in proper alignment with the Creator. We aren't designed to be good fathers or husbands outside of our connection with our Creator. I believe men who understand that it is their responsibility to lead, provide for, and protect their families frequently feel the pressure and weight of their responsibility in their roles as husbands and fathers. Men who attempt to fulfill these roles outside of God and in their own power and understanding, often find themselves experiencing the greatest amount of frustration and stress. Before the Fall, when Adam was in perfect spiritual alignment with his Creator, Adam and Eve's lives were a literal cakewalk. After the Fall, when Adam was out of spiritual alignment with his Creator and experienced being kicked out of the Garden as a result of his sin, life was made hard and frustrating for both Adam and Eve (Genesis 3:16-19).

Now that I have established what it means to be God's man in the context of the family: a mature husband or father is one who understands and embraces his biblical responsibility to function as the loving and compassionate leader of his home, who provides for and protects his wife and children in ways that reflect their differing relationships, I will spend the next several chapters expounding on what leading, providing, and protecting looks like in the biblical sense, and how we can best model the biblical blueprint of manhood that God has laid out in His Word.

Footnotes

1   Piper, John. "A Vision of Biblical Complementarity." *Recovering Biblical Manhood and Womanhood: A Response to Evangelical Feminism.* Ed. John Piper and Wayne Grudem. Wheaton, Illinois: Crossway, 2006 (Second Edition). 31-59.

2   I believe John Piper provides an excellent (but quite broad) definition of mature manhood/masculinity that applies to all men including married and single men and men with and without children. The definition I provide is more specific to mature manhood as it relates to husbands and fathers and more closely parallels to the purpose and intent of this book.

PART II

Leading Your Family God's Way

Let's be real. Men have the capacity to lead. Steve Jobs, one of the co-founders of Apple Inc., and arguably the father of modern technology, helped catapult Apple from a local start-up company housed in his parent's garage, into the 600 billion dollar multinational giant that we know and love today. Mahatma Gandhi, one of the most influential religious and political leaders of our time, led India colonized under British rule to liberation and independence through mass non-violent protests and civil disobedience. President Abraham Lincoln, the sixteenth president of the United States, led our country through its bloodiest war—the Civil War— and initiated the eventual dismantling of nearly two hundred and fifty years of American slavery. Finally, Michael "Air" Jordan who led the National Basketball Association in scoring an unprecedented ten times, propelled the Chicago Bulls to six championships in a single decade, and headlined the 1992 gold medal winning U.S. Basketball Team. This team, forever written in history books as the "Dream Team," was arguably the best Olympic basketball team we have ever seen, and perhaps will ever see, defeating opponents by an average of nearly 44 points a game. The point is, men know how to lead. That is not the problem. Men lead in a variety of capacities and do it well. The problem is, men seldom lead to their full potential in the arena where leading counts the most, and that is, within the context of the family. It's my contention that it's not that men don't want to lead in their homes, we just often have few models, and as a consequence, frequently find ourselves struggling to lead our families effectively.

MANHOOD: FOLLOWING THE BLUEPRINT OF GOD'S WORD

One of the most important lessons that I would like men to take from this book is that although we frequently struggle with our identities as husbands and fathers, all is not lost. There is hope, and we are not left without help. Listen up! Yes, YOU. If your

Bible is nearby, grab it. Whether you use the old-fashioned, 1000-page, red-letter King James Bible, an iPad, smart phone, or some other device, go ahead and grab it. Lift it up to Heaven and say these words: "I might not have it all figured out, but thank God for HIS instructions!"

Now I know as men we rarely like to follow directions. But as Dr. Phil often says: "How is that working for you?" Proverbs 19:20 states: "Get all the advice and instruction you can, so you will be wise the rest of your life" (NLT). What better advisor than God Himself? What better set of instructions than the Word of God? God's Word presents a clear set of biblical principles that define what effective and mature male leadership looks like in the context of the family, and a clear blueprint to how husbands and fathers should operate and function on the earth. Given the clarity of God's Word, we should father and husband our families with a clear goal in mind: to follow the blueprint laid out in God's Word.

We don't become good fathers or husbands by chance; we have to put in the time and effort to study the blueprint and faithfully model it in our lives. Nor do we fully become men in the sense of perfection. Rather, like the sanctification process, manhood is a lifetime call—a lifetime striving. As we strive to look more and more like Christ, we begin to conform more and more into the masculine image that God originally designed us to reflect. Since the Fall, males have been striving (struggling) to do whatever they can to make it in this world. It should come as no surprise then that the process to become the man that God has called you to be will look more like a marathon and less like a sprint.

BECOMING GOD'S MAN: OBTAINING THE PRIZE, ENJOYING THE BENEFITS

To become a good man, in general, and a good husband or father, in particular, we need to run the marathon of life with a specific goal or prize in mind. First Corinthians 9:24 states: "Do you not know that those who run in a race all run, but only one receives the prize? Run in such a way that you may win" (NASB). I believe great leaders like Steve Jobs, Mahatma Gandhi, Abraham Lincoln, and Michael Jordan ran the race of their lives with a specific goal or prize in mind: to win. How else were they so wildly successful in their lifetimes? As one sports commentator suggested, what made Michael Jordan great and not good was that the only thing he felt more passionately about than winning, was not losing. I'm not suggesting that our primary motivation for being good leaders in our home should be fear, but rather our eye has to be fixed on the prize. Each season Michael Jordan lived for winning. Great leaders are driven by success. As husbands and fathers, we need to be driven by the benefits of success. We should be driven to become better leaders of our homes because there are great benefits to doing things God's way.

When we make God's Word the foundation of what we do as husbands and fathers and allow God to conform our marriages and families to His image and not our own the benefits are: happy and healthy marriages, spiritually and emotionally well-balanced children, and a family unit that knows their purpose and function in this world and in God's Kingdom. I don't know about you, but count me in! So what is the prize in the context of this section of the book? It is to become the husbands and fathers that we are called to be. To become men who "understand and embrace our biblical responsibility to function as loving and compassionate leaders of our homes, who provide for and protect their wives and children in ways that reflect their differing relationships."

GODLY HUSBANDS AS INITIATORS AND IMITATORS

I believe there are at least two dimensions of mature male leadership in the family that I would like to highlight and discuss in-depth throughout this section. Good husbands are first, *imitators* of the attributes of Christ as their marriages reflect the same relationship that Christ has with His church (Ephesians 5:22-23) (Chapter 4). Biblically mature husbands and or fathers are also imitators of Christ in that they display love and compassion towards their wives and children (Chapter 5) and are servant-leaders of their homes (Chapter 6). In other words, mature husbands and or fathers are committed to *loving* like Christ, *leading* like Christ, and are *willing to die* for their wives and children, just like Christ (Ephesians 5:25-29). Second, mature husbands and fathers are *initiators* who set the tone and environment of their home (Chapter 7). Mature husbands and fathers fully embrace these two dimensions (imitating and initiating) and are committed to developing these attributes in their lives.

In over thirty years of counseling and work in ministry, I have witnessed these two biblical principles successfully at work in hundreds of marriages, including my own. If you truly want to grow as a leader and see your marriage and family life bloom, become a tone setter of your home through demonstrating a pattern of initiation (leading by example) and faithfully modeling the personality and leadership style of Christ as a loving and compassionate servant-leader in the home.

CHAPTER 4 —————

Divine Imitators: God, Marriage, and Male Headship

In many Bibles, the sub-heading for the fifth chapter of Ephesians is "Be Imitators of God." This subheading takes us back to the first several chapters of Genesis, and reminds us that we were and are created in the very image of God. The problem is, we frequently mirror the lust and selfish inclinations of our own flesh more than we reflect the image of a Holy God. Leaving our past life and inclinations behind, the Apostle Paul begins the fifth chapter of Ephesians with these words: "Therefore be imitators of God, as beloved children; and walk in love, just as Christ also loved you and gave himself up for us, an offering and sacrifice to God as a fragrant aroma" (Ephesians 5:1-2). To put things in their proper context, Paul outlines in the prior chapter what Christian conduct should look like both in the Body of Christ (Ephesians 4:1-16) and in our personal walk (Ephesians 4:17-32). In the fifth chapter of Ephesians, Paul turns his attention to marriage. He writes in Ephesians 5:22-24:

> Wives, be subject to your own husbands, as to the Lord. For the husband is the head of the wife, as Christ also is the head of the church, He himself being the Savior of the body. But as the church is subject to Christ, so also the wives ought to be to their husbands in everything.

In other words, marriage between one man and one woman should reflect Christ's relationship with the church. As God the Father has placed Christ as the head of the universal body of believers (The Church), He also positions husbands as the head of their wives and families. Christ is the "head" leader and lead authority figure of the church. Husbands in like manner, are authorized by God to be the "heads" and leaders of their families. Furthermore, wives are called to submit (in the Greek: *hupotasso)* or to be subject to their husbands. Submission in this way manifests itself to the degree to which a wife honors or respects her husband (Ephesians 5:33). In Paul's words, wives are to submit to their husbands "as unto the Lord." In other words, when wives dishonor their husbands they essentially dishonor God. As Romans 13:2 states: "...whoever rebels against the authority is rebelling against what God has instituted, and those who do so will bring judgment on themselves" (NIV). Does this mean that husbands are or take the place of the Lord in their marriages? God forbid, of course not! As John Piper argues:

> The analogy between Christ and the husband breaks down if pressed too far, first because, unlike Christ, all men sin. Christ never has to apologize to his church. But husbands must do this often. Moreover, unlike Christ, a husband is not preparing a bride merely for himself but for another, namely Christ. He does not merely act as Christ, but also for Christ...[he must reject] the temptation to be Christ [to his wife]. And that means leading his wife forward to depend not on him but on Christ (p. 38).[1]

Husbands are not Christ and should never attempt to take the place of Christ in their marriages. Nor should husbands lead their wives and children to depend on them in a spiritual sense, but rather they should see to it that they trust the Lord in and through everything. This is extremely important because as a husband there will be times when you may let your wife down, you may not have all the answers, or you may not have the words to say to encourage her. In these instances, husbands need to lead their wives forward to trust in a perfect and Holy God Who fully understands what we go through and experience on a daily basis, and has the power to change our situation (Hebrews 4:14-16).

If wives desire to honor and please God in their marriages they will give their husbands unconditional respect. Unconditional respect and honoring looks like remaining in alignment with and following the direction of your husband even when you don't understand or agree with his decision as long as it isn't illegal or ungodly (1 Corinthians 11:1). This looks like looking past one's husband's weaknesses, insecurities, and flaws; and instead honoring their position, their authority and direction for the family. This also looks like refusing to usurp or undermine their authority and acknowledging that you honor and appreciate their leadership and desire to support and follow them to the best of your ability. In doing so, wives honor God.

You're probably saying that this is doable if your husband knows the Lord, but what if he doesn't? Should I still submit to him and respect his authority? The Apostle Peter has a word to you, too. The principle of submission and unconditional respect are still in play. First Peter 3:1 states:

Wives, in the same way submit yourselves to your own husbands so that, if any of them do not believe the word (are an unbeliever), they may be won over without words by the behavior of their wives (NIV).

Peter communicates here that respect and honor in the context of husband-wife relations are not conditional in the sense that husbands are only to be respected when they are "worthy" or "deserving" of it based on a wife's perspective or opinion, but rather on the husband's position in the family (1 Peter 2:13-14; Romans 13:1-2). Even when a husband is an unbeliever, you still need to respect his position in your life. If you prove yourself to be a Godly wife to him through your words and deeds as a woman of God, Peter says that you will "win" your spouse for Christ with your virtuous and Christ-like behavior. This biblical principle demonstrates that as the saved spouse you should properly reflect the image of God and stand as the "light" and "salt" in your marriage (Matthew 5:14-16). You are to follow your husband's leadership as unto the Lord (Ephesians 5:22; 1 Corinthians 11:1). When your husband's leading contradicts God's Word you are not obligated to follow, but you are expected to resist his rebellion in a way that does not disrespect his authority. As Pastor

John Piper highlights:

[A wife] must never follow her husband's leadership into sin. She [should] not steal with him or get drunk with him or savor pornography with him or develop deceptive schemes with him...but even where a Christian wife may have to stand with Christ against the sinful will of her husband, she can still have a spirit of submission – a disposition to yield. She can show by her attitude and behavior that she does not like resisting his will and that she longs for him to resist sin and lead in righteousness so that her disposition to honor him as head can again produce harmony (pg. 47).[2]

Wives should never follow their husbands down the path of sin and rebellion. Such a choice does not reflect biblical submission and dishonors God. Likewise, it dishonors God to tear down one's husband with their words when he is living in sin or struggling with his relationship with God. In a practical sense, if your husband is a believer and he comes home late at night intoxicated, it dishonors God for a wife to berate him by telling him that he's "a horrible excuse for a man," that he is "good for nothing," "…ain't nothing and never will be nothing," or that he's "just like his daddy." These women are operating outside of the will of God by discouraging and tearing down what God has placed in their lives to encourage and build up. Instead, wives who properly stand with God against their husband's sin, do so with a loving and encouraging demeanor that affirms and honors his position as head of the family, but respectfully resists his disposition to dishonor God.

Finally, God's ideal marriage is one where both husband and wife are believers and are led by the Holy Spirit. Godly marriages shouldn't be one-sided in the sense that wives or husbands pour out of themselves, getting nothing back in return. The Apostle Paul stresses the importance of mutual submission in marriage where husbands love and cherish their wives unconditionally, and wives in turn, respect and honor their husbands unconditionally (Ephesians 5:33). In this type of marriage, husband-wife relationships and roles are complementary, and are designed for both spouses to get what they need. Husbands feel honored and respected, and wives feel honored and cherished.

Male-Female Equality. Male headship is frequently misunderstood. Many believe that because men are called to be the head of their households, God, somehow, views them as "superior" or "superhuman" relative to the weaker (perhaps inferior) and less-valued women. This couldn't be further from the truth. In his article titled, "Male-Female Equality and Male Headship," Pastor Raymond C. Ortlund, Jr., describes male headship in the following way: "In the partnership of two spiritually equal human beings (man and woman), the man bears the primary responsibility to lead the partnership in a God-glorifying direction."[3]

I've already discussed in earlier chapters that Adam and Eve were both created in the image of God, they were equally blessed and commanded to co-rule the earth. The first several chapters of Genesis makes clear that God viewed (and continues to view) men and women of equal worth and as spiritual equals insofar that men and women are fellow-heirs in eternal life, and there is neither male or female in Christ (Galatians 3:28). In this God-glorifying relationship however, God calls the husband to lead and give account for the moral-spiritual life of the family (Genesis 3:9). Notice that husbands should lead their wives and families in a way that glorifies God. Husbands who make demands or attempt to bulldoze control or manipulate their wives do not reflect the demeanor and attributes of Christ. These men abuse their position as the head of their households. God ordained husbands to model loving and compassionate leadership in their homes (male headship). This form of loving leadership should be contrasted with abusive forms of leadership that deviate from the Word of God (such as male domination). Men who through compulsion or manipulation force their will over their wives and reflect an abusive demeanor with their words and actions don't reflect biblical male headship, but rather male domination. These husbands disregard or neglect altogether that their wives are of equal worth and deserve respect and unconditional love. Male headship is God's divine order for male-female relations in marriage; male domination is an unhealthy distortion/corruption of husband-wife relations since the fall (Genesis 3:16). But male headship is only properly modeled when husbands love their wives like Christ loves the church (Ephesians 5:25).

WHAT ABOUT WIVES?

Although husbands are to take the primary leadership position in the family, this does not mean that wives have no responsibility at all. God also created Eve with a unique set of roles and responsibilities within the context of the family. Genesis 2:18 states: "Then the Lord said it is not good for man to be alone; I will make him a helper suitable for him" (NASB). The word "alone" here can best be interpreted as "a companion of his kind or likeness." Every animal in the Garden had a Mr. and Mrs., but Adam had no one to relate to on his level. The terms *helper* and *suitable* suggest that Eve's purpose was to help and assist (*ezer*) Adam and that she would be a suitable companion who was his opposite-equal (*neged*). By opposite-equal it is implied that Eve was created to be his equal in the sense that she was a perfect companion. She was also opposite of him in the sense that she was of opposite sex and had a distinct role and set of responsibilities in the relationship. As Adam's opposite-equal companion, it was Eve's function to assist or help Adam.

Now, I know that many of the wives and future wives who are reading this book are probably saying to themselves: "Now, you mean to tell me that as a wife I need to drop everything for my husband?" "Really, I have to forget about all of my plans, dreams, goals, and aspirations?" "Are you kidding me, my education becomes irrelevant once I get married, and my desires have to take a backseat?" The problem lies in how we view the word "helper." When we think of the word helper we think servant, maid, or doormat. We think of a woman who is without power or has little power. Thoughts of women as second-class citizens with little value or worth also come to mind. I understand (and, men, you should understand) that for many women their greatest fear is getting married and losing their selves and their identity; having to give it all up for their husbands and children. Ladies, if I told you that you were needed to "assist" or "help" at a growing Fortune 500 company, and that I needed you to be second-in-command with a starting salary of $10.5 million dollars a year, would it make you feel like a second-class citizen? More than likely, you would be happy to step into that role and cash your checks every week. Why? Although you were asked to be a help or support, the position is considered one of honor and prestige. Being a wife is often considered unglamorous. But when God designed Eve as a suitable helper to Adam, I don't believe that is what He intended.

The Hebrew word for helper also has another meaning that I wish to communicate. In the Hebrew, the word *ezer* also means one who helps, assists, and supports, especially during hard or difficult times. The word *ezer* appears 21 times in the Old Testament. In every instance except for the two in Genesis that refer to Eve, the word is used to describe the help and support we get from God (see Deuteronomy 33:7, Psalm 33:20, Psalm 70:5 for examples). I am not at all suggesting that wives are to help or assist men in the same manner that God does. But what I am suggesting is that to be a helper or *ezer* isn't necessarily negative. It also connotes a unique power and strength that wives bring to the marriage to support and assist their husbands as they strive to be all they are called to be as men. This is an honor, not a curse. It's easy to focus on wives as "helpers" and overlook the point that MEN NEED HELP.

I believe that God's intention for marriage is that husbands take the lead (head). In this role, men bear the primary responsibility and burden of the family on his shoulders. As a husband, it is also his responsibility to "help" or "assist" his wife become all that she is called to be through nourishing (helping her grow to maturity) and cherishing her (giving her unconditional love and care) (Ephesians 5:30). Likewise, it is the wife's primary responsibility to "help" or "assist" her husband by responding to his leadership, by affirming and nurturing his strength, and by showing him unconditional honor and respect (Ephesians 5:33).

WOMEN, THE FAMILY, WORK, AND FULFILLMENT

One of the biggest concerns of many women today is: Can I be fulfilled as a wife and/or mother? Ask corporately successful women whom you admire whether they sense a feeling of fulfillment in their lives. The reality is, many women who are corporately successful do not sense a feeling of complete or total fulfillment. I am not saying that women cannot find fulfillment in their careers; some may. But men get a different fulfillment from their work than women do.

As a pastor and trained counselor for many years, I've encountered countless married corporate and professional mothers who enjoy their jobs, but experience work and family conflict in their roles as workers, wives, and mothers. These women frequently express a great deal of stress and guilt as they climb up the corporate ladder and find themselves less able to devote the time and energy that they desire to their husbands and children. Find me a husband and father who is corporately successful. That same man more than likely finds fulfillment and pride in his ability to earn a living that supplies his family with financial security and a lifestyle that he desires them to have. This isn't a sexist description of male-female work/family fulfillment dynamics. It is a reality of God's divine plan for how men and women were to function since creation. God ordains for women to find fulfillment in their home life and men to find fulfillment in their work/career.

The second and third chapters of Genesis highlight the differing roles and responsibilities that God ordained for Adam and Eve to occupy in the context of the family. Adam was given the responsibility to provide for the needs of his family by laboring in the Garden with his hands (Genesis 2:15). Eve, on the other hand, was given the responsibility to be a helper to her husband and care for the needs of the family in the domain of the home (Genesis 2:18). As Adam's opposite-equal, it wasn't until Eve came on the scene that Adam was able to fulfill God's mandate to be "fruitful and multiply" (Genesis 1:22).

God was so serious about the differing roles and responsibilities of males and females that when He cursed Adam and Eve after the Fall He cursed them in their specific domains or spheres of work or influence. For Adam, He cursed the ground saying:

> ...since you listened to your wife and ate from the tree whose fruit I commanded you not to eat, the ground is cursed because of you. All your life you will struggle to scratch a living from it. It will grow thorns and thistles for you...by the sweat of your brow [hard physical labor] will you have food to eat (Genesis 3:17-19, NLT).

For Eve, God multiplied her labor pain in childbirth saying: "I will sharpen the pain of your pregnancy, and in pain you will give birth. And you will desire to control [or to take your husband's position of authority] but he will rule over you" (Genesis 3:16, NLT). Although we frequently put a value on these differing spheres of work, it is important to note that both were essential for the effective functioning and livelihood of the family. It is clear from the manner in which God cursed Adam and Eve that it was God's original intent and plan that Adam and

Eve live and function in a complementary manner. It was Adam's (men) biblical responsibility to take the leadership role in providing for the financial and material needs by working in the Garden. On the contrary, it was Eve's purpose to be a "helper" to Adam and to care for the needs of the home environment as wife and mother.

When our marriages follow this order, when we, as husbands and wives, are engrossed in meeting each other's needs in a biblical sense, husbands will get what they need and will become all that God has called them to be, and wives will get what they need and will become all that God has called them to be. We both are fulfilled. We both win. There are no losers and nothing lacking.

Footnotes

1   Piper, John. "A Vision of Biblical Complementarity." *Recovering Biblical Manhood and Womanhood: A Response to Evangelical Feminism.* Ed. John Piper and Wayne Grudem. Wheaton, Illinois: Crossway, 2006 (Second Edition). 31-59.

2   See Note 1

3   Ortlund, Raymond. C. "Male-Female Equality and Male Headship: Genesis 1-3." *Recovering Biblical Manhood and Womanhood: A Response to Evangelical Feminism.* Ed. John Piper and Wayne Grudem. Wheaton, Illinois: Crossway, 2006 (Second Edition). 31-59.

CHAPTER 5 ─────────────

Loving and Compassionate Leaders of the Home

Before we can learn how to lead as husbands and fathers, we must first learn how to love. In the previous section of this book, I put forth a working definition of what a good man looks like in the context of the family: "Mature husbands and fathers are men who understand and embrace their biblical responsibility to function as loving and compassionate leaders of their home, who provide for and protect their wives and children in ways that reflect their differing relationships." In this chapter, the key phrase is that mature husbands and fathers understand their biblical responsibility to function as "loving and compassionate leaders of their home."

THE CHALLENGE

Here's the challenge: societal conceptualizations of masculinity are distorted. Most men have been taught that emotions like love and compassion are feminine traits and make men less of a man. We've been told that men are strong and honorable and I would certainly agree that we should be. We've probably also heard our entire lives that men should never display emotions, that they should never appear to be weak or vulnerable in the presence of others; and we've embraced these notions of masculinity as truth. The unfortunate result is that we have a generation of husbands and fathers who are emotionally unavailable and disconnected from their wives and children.

Listen, my brother, we will never be the husbands and fathers that God has called us to be, nor will our families ever reach their full potential and purpose in the Kingdom, unless we are committed to imitating the image of Christ and rejecting the image of masculinity that the world has placed on us. The Apostle Paul says it this way: "And do not be conformed to this world, but be transformed by the renewing of your mind, so that you may prove what the will of God is, that which is good and acceptable and perfect" (Romans 12:2, NASB). In other words, if our desire is to be in the perfect will of God and to move our family to His will, we cannot make the mistake of copying the behaviors and customs of this world. Instead, we should imitate or conform to the mind and behavior of Christ.

I believe that we imitate Christ as husbands and fathers by first *loving like Christ* and modeling the love that Christ demonstrates towards us. Second, we imitate our Savior by *leading like Christ* and following the type of leadership that Christ modeled while on earth. Third, we imitate Christ by demonstrating our willingness to *die or sacrifice like Christ*. In other words, we are committed to showing our wives and children that we are willing to lay down our lives for them; putting their needs before our own.

LOVING LIKE CHRIST

Christ's love for us isn't anything like we've ever seen or experienced. Romans 5:8 states: "...God demonstrates his own love for us, in that while we were yet sinners, Christ died for us." In the above Scripture, the Apostle Paul highlights the fact that Christ made a decision to die for us (take our place on the cross) even when we were in our very worst state (while we yet sinners). In other words, Christ's love for us is not based on our goodness; it is based on His goodness. Another way to state this is that Christ's love for us is unconditional. In the original language of the text (Greek), the word love here is "agape" which refers to unconditional love that both originates and flows from God. This is the same term that Paul uses when he says to husbands in Ephesians 5:28-30: "So husbands ought also to *love* their own wives as their own bodies. He who loves his own wife loves himself; for no one ever hated his own flesh, but *nourishes* and *cherishes* it, just as Christ also does the church."

LOVING YOUR WIFE GOD'S WAY: TO NOURISH AND CHERISH

In Ephesians 5:28-30, the Apostle Paul uses the analogy that as Christ is the head of the universal body of believers, so also are husbands the head of their own wives. In both cases, the head and the body are joined together by a covenant or formally sealed binding relationship. As Christ and His church are one in the context of a covenant, a husband and wife are one (flesh). In this way, to love one's own wife is analogous to loving one's own self (body). The Apostle Paul continues: "he who loves his own wife loves himself; for no one ever hated his own flesh, but *nourishes* and *cherishes* it" (Ephesians 5:29).

In the original language of the text, the word "nourish" or *Ektrepho* can best be translated as to nourish up to maturity, to nurture and bring up. The word "cherish" or *Thalpo* means to cherish with tender love and care. In other words, it is our biblical responsibility as husbands to cherish our wives with our words and actions, demonstrating our tender love and care for them. Furthermore, it is also our responsibility to nourish them as we would our own bodies, helping them to mature and to reach their full potential. In other words, it is our responsibility as the leaders of our home to grow spiritually so that we can, in turn, support and facilitate our wives' spiritual growth process. We must guide our wives to answer the divine call and purpose on their own lives. We should encourage our wives to reach for the stars and pursue their dreams.

When our wives struggle with their faith or trusting God, it's crucial that we encourage them in a non-condemning way to trust God and stand firm on His Word. We must be committed to building our wives up and careful not to tear her down. We should view our wives as precious gifts from God who deserve our unconditional love, honor, and respect. Our wives deserve to be nurtured and cherished not simply because of what they do or do not do, but because they are fellow-heirs of the Kingdom God. As Peter states: "...husbands...live with your wives in an understanding way, as with someone (physically and perhaps emotionally more fragile) weaker, since she is a woman; and show her honor as a fellow heir of the grace of life, so that your prayers will not be hindered" (1 Peter 3:7).

Whether we realize it or not, our wives are daughters of the Most High. When we mistreat her, neglect her or abuse her, her heavenly Father will expect us to give an account of our actions and make things right. In fact, God takes our love and care for His daughters so seriously, that when we fail to nourish and cherish our wives the Word says, "...our prayers will be hindered." Imagine that, when we neglect or refuse to cherish one of God's precious daughters, His response is that He shuts up Heaven and stops listening to our prayers until we make things right. Our wives are like delicate flowers. It's so important that we create an environment in our home that allows them to grow and flourish. Like a beautiful flower, our nourishment, encouragement and tender love and care plays a crucial role in their spiritual growth and development.

MODELING LOVING LEADERSHIP

As highlighted earlier, loving male leadership reflects agape or unconditional love, and is seasoned with a commitment to show our wives that we are committed to giving them tender love and care. In this way, mature male leadership rules out belligerent, authoritative, non-compromising and dictatorial forms of husbanding and fatherhood. Husbands and fathers are not commanded to rule their homes with an iron fist; they are commanded to love and be sensitive leaders who model the demeanor of Christ. When we lead in this way, we lead our families with their best interest at heart and from the posture of compassion and unconditional love and support. In other words, we need to love our wives and children with the love of Christ. We must love them with unconditional love that is not based on their goodness, but based on God's goodness. To love our wives with unconditional love is to love them (show them love) even when they are behaving in an unloving way. In a biblical sense, as husbands, we do not have the right, nor are we justified in deciding whether our wives are *worthy* of our love or affection moment to moment.

THE POWER OF YOUR ACTIONS

True love manifesting in the heart of a husband, will seek to find and understand the things that he can do for his wife to make her feel loved and appreciated. One of the most powerful questions that you can ask a woman is what can I do for you today? What is your most pressing need? To do so, you will hear the innermost thoughts of your wife, and if you respond properly to that need, your wife will feel loved in that moment. It's not good enough to assume your wife knows that you love her because you've been married for nineteen years, you work sixty hours a week, or because you clean her car on every second and fourth Saturday. If you want to show your wife that you love her, begin by finding out what makes her feel loved, cherished and special, and then begin to do those things.

THE POWER OF YOUR WORDS

In addition to what we do (our actions), we also set the tone and environment in our households and families by what we say (our words). Proverbs 18:21a (KJV) states that: "Death and life are in the power of the tongue…" By virtue of our position in the family as the designated head, we are authorized to speak over and speak into the lives of our wives and children. In marriage, God ordains husbands to be initiators and wives (and children) are built to respond to their initiation. Whether we realize it or not, the heart of our wives is like a bank. Whatever we sow into them (whether positive or negative) we will always get back in return. Galatians 6:7 (NASB) states: "Do not be deceived, God is not mocked; for whatever a man sows, this he will also reap." Words of encouragement, love, support, and affirmation are like deposits that fill the vault of their hearts. On the contrary, when we tear down our wives with words of discouragement, rejection, and negativity we make withdrawals from the vaults of our wives' hearts. Just as in a bank, if we make too many withdrawals and not enough deposits, eventually our wives' hearts will become bankrupt, our wives will become bitter and miserable and the tone and environment of our homes will begin to sour.

I've learned in my own marriage the benefits and the power of my words to set the tone and environment of my household. Earlier in my marriage, my wife and I had many heated verbal battles. However, as we grew together, and I discovered that whatever I projected or threw at my wife, I always got it back in return, I began to speak life and not death to my wife and demonstrate my unconditional love and care for her through my words and I witnessed our home environment transform positively. Now it's not to say that my wife and I don't have disagreements—every once in a while it goes down in the Henderson household. When we do, however, my wife doesn't call me out of my name because I don't call her out of hers. Nor do I degrade my wife, treat her like a child or some type of object and she doesn't project that back to me.

On the contrary, I've come to the realization that as

the king of my home, my wife should be treated like a queen. She deserves to feel like a queen. I make a point to affirm my wife, to tell her how much I love her, to tell her how attractive she is, and to let her know that she is a wonderful mother and ministry partner. One of her favorite pastimes is to shop. I enjoy listening to her talk about a new dress or pair of shoes that she found at one of her favorite stores. When she comes home I love asking her to try it on and show me what she's working with. As the initiator of my home, my wife rarely leaves the house without me telling her how good she looks, how much I love her, or how important she is in my life. I want to be the first voice of affirmation and love that my wife hears before she even leaves the house. Believe me brother, if you want to turn your wife on, learn how to speak life and not death into and over her life. Learn to shower her with the power of your words. Be intentional about making more deposits than withdrawals. I promise you, your commitment to encourage your wife, will return great dividends.

The mistake many men make is to assume that their wives should know that they love them by what they do for them. That's important, but sometimes our wives need to hear how much we care. Adam established in the beginning with great joy and excitement that God fashioned a companion who was perfectly suitable and designed with him in mind.

Undoubtedly, the first wedding vow, Adam acknowledged before God and Eve that he was committed to forsake all others to be joined to his bride. The word "joined" or "cleave" in the King James Version derives from the Hebrew word *dabaq*, which means to cling to, to keep close to one's self, to stick together, to remain steadfast, and to closely pursue. I believe Adam was expressing that his commitment to Eve was so resolute and life-long, that he was bent on pursuing Eve's heart for the rest of his days. Fellas, if you really want to elicit a response from your wife and demonstrate a pattern of initiation in your marriage with your words, let her know that you will *dabaq* her for the rest of your days on the earth.

CHAPTER 6 —————

Servant-Leaders of the Home

Although Christ by virtue of His position and who He was and is (God) had every right to come to earth reigning as a king exercising His authority over the people of this earth, He chose, instead, to humble Himself. Speaking to the Church of Philippi, the Apostle Paul says the following about Christ: "...Christ Jesus, who, although He existed in the form of God, did not regard equality with God a thing to be grasped, but instead emptied Himself, taking the form of a bond-servant [or servant]...and being found in appearance as a man, He humbled Himself by becoming obedient to the point of death even death on a cross."

The beauty of Christ's leadership style is that He never

demanded to be served while on this earth; instead He humbled Himself and made it His priority to serve others (see also Matthew 20:26-28; Mark 10:43-45). Luke 22:24-27 also provides an excellent example of Jesus' expectations for His disciples and future followers. In these verses, a great dispute or argument arose among the disciples regarding which one of them were the greatest. Jesus expressed to them the world's way of doing things is very different from the Kingdom's. In the world, leaders ruled over others and exercised authority over their subjects. But in the Kingdom, great men lead by example, and lived their lives to serve those they were over. Jesus pointed to Himself as the model for great leadership by saying: "For who is greater, the one who reclines at the table or the one who serves? Is it not the one who reclines at the table? But I am among you [the greatest that was, the greatest that will ever be] as the one who serves" (Luke 22:27). Afterward, Jesus got up from the supper, laying aside His garment and taking a towel, He wrapped it around His waist. Then He began to wash His disciples' feet. When He was finished, Jesus went back to the table saying: "Do you know what I have done to you? You call Me Teacher and Lord; and you are right, for so I am. If I then, the Lord and the Teacher, washed your feet, you also ought to wash one another's feet. For I gave you an example that you also should do as I did to you…if you know these things, you are blessed if you do them" (John 13:12-15, 17, NASB).

Consider the fact that foot washing was an important hospitality custom during the time of Jesus. People often traveled by foot and used sandals as their primary footwear. Given this fact, one's feet were generally the dirtiest part of one's body after a long day's journey. In most cases, especially in the homes of great men, men of authority or distinction would arrange for their servants to prepare the water for and wash the feet of their guest. In this instance, Jesus prepared the water and washed the feet of each of His disciples Himself, showing them by example that great leaders, lead by example and make it a priority to serve others. In like manner, husbands should follow the pattern laid out by Christ. Husbands should not demand to be served by virtue of their position as the head of their families and household, rather they need to lead by example by serving their families with the demeanor and attitude of Christ. Christ's demeanor was one of servant-leadership.

SACRIFICING LIKE CHRIST

As husbands and fathers we are also called to sacrifice or die like Christ and put our families' needs before our own. The latter part of Ephesians 5:25 communicates for husbands to love their wives, like Christ loves the church: "…[giving] himself up for her, so that He might sanctify her, having cleansed her by the washing of water with the word, that He might present to Himself the church in all her glory, having no spot or wrinkle or any such thing; but that she would be holy and blameless" (NASB).

Husbands are to first and foremost be willing to give up of themselves for their wives and children, which looks like putting their wives and children's needs and interests before their own. This is a call to be selfless and to serve your family with the heart of a humble servant. True love gives expecting nothing in return. Remember that God's love (agape) isn't simply unconditional; it is also self-sacrificing in the sense that: "God so loved the world that he *gave* his one and only son, so that everyone who believes in him will not perish but have eternal life" (John 3:16, NIV). True love is expressed in that Christ by virtue of His position and authority as almighty God (Isaiah 9:6) had every right to reign while on earth, but He came down wrapped up in flesh to die, so that we could live (Romans 5:8; Philippians 2:8). Likewise, we learn in Scripture that Christ, our living savior still has our best interests at heart as he intercedes (prays) for us daily as our high priest (Hebrews 7:23-25). "But because Jesus lives forever, his priesthood last forever...he lives forever to intercede with God on [our] behalf (NLT)." This is symbolic in the sense that Christ died for us once and for all, making us his priority and preferring us to himself. Nonetheless, Jesus, as our high priest, continues to die daily interceding on our behalf and making us his priority.

Like Jesus, we are the high priests of our households. There was nothing glamorous about the jobs of high priests. It was bloody, often involved the cutting of flesh and much sacrifice. Likewise, being a Godly husband requires much sacrifice; it is a bloody and un-glamorous job at times and requires the cutting of (our own) flesh. Not only do we need to put our wives and children's needs before our own. We need to be willing to die for them and willing to allow our flesh to die daily for their sake? What I mean by this is sometimes we need to hold our tongue — not say everything on our mind in the middle of an argument. Although its difficult, sometimes we need to allow our wives to have the last word or be willing to not have to always say that we are right. Sometimes being a high priest looks like sacrificing our pride for a spirit of meekness or allowing the fruit of the spirit to be made manifest our lives.

Loving our wives and children like Christ is not something that we can do on our own. We need to rely on Christ as our source to conform us to his image and receive his love so that we can in turn pour it out on our wives and children. Love after all, is a fruit of the spirit (Galatians 5:22). How else can we truly love with the unconditional love of Christ without the Holy Spirit (of Christ) indwelling inside of us? The Apostle John described the Holy Spirit as a daily helper and guide that will teach us all things and direct us in all truth (John 14:16, 26; John 16:13).

As a child if we played basketball, little league baseball or any sport for that matter, we understand that sometimes we have to "be the man" and take one for the team if you want to win the game. Being self-sacrificial looks like putting your families needs and interest above your own, extending grace when necessary and not reacting but rather responding in love at all times. That is what "taking one for the team really looks like." If you are willing to do that my brother, YOU THA' MAN!

CHAPTER 7 ——————

Getting Schooled by God: Lessons from a Divine Initiator

When we consider God's relationship with mankind in Genesis, it is quite clear that part of God's nature is that He is an initiator. To initiate is to lead by example, to set the tone and expectations of a relationship or interaction. In this sense, God established the tone and nature of His relationship with mankind from the very beginning. In particular, God made it a priority to clearly establish the expectations and boundaries by which Adam was supposed to live. God gave Adam an assignment or job (Genesis 2:15) and gave him direction on which trees were acceptable and unacceptable to eat from (Genesis 2:16-17).

Perhaps the greatest demonstration of God's personality as an initiator occurs when He brings every living creature on the earth to Adam to see what he would call them (Genesis 2:19). Like a loving father showing his son all that he made for him, God empowers Adam to name the animals one by one (Genesis 2:19). It's easy to dismiss this moment as a business as usual phase of creation, but what God was doing was much more intentional. God was empowering Adam to function in the authority that He had already commanded him to walk in. Perhaps even greater, God was teaching Adam to take initiative. To name the animals was an act of authority and God bringing each animal to Adam one by one was demonstration of each animal's subjection to Adam's God-given delegated authority. God wanted Adam to know what it was like to have responsibility, to lead and make decisions.

By Genesis 2:23 (NASB), it's clear that Adam learned the lesson. When God brought Eve to him, God didn't even need to prompt Adam to name Eve; he took the initiative upon himself and said: "This is now bone of my bones, and flesh of my flesh; she shall be called *woman* because she was taken out of man." Adam followed the pattern of initiation that God laid out. God established the rules and boundaries of His relationship with mankind, giving Adam an identity, an assignment or job, and the spiritual expectations for life.

Adam properly responded to God's leadership and initiative by establishing the rules and boundaries of his relationship with Eve. After God creates Eve and brings her to Adam, Adam responds in Genesis 2:24 (NASB) by saying: "...For this reason a man shall leave his father and his mother, and be joined to his wife; and they shall become one flesh." Genesis 2:23-24 demonstrates that Adam learned how to follow and quickly learned from God's lead and pattern of initiation. God is a divine initiator, and as husbands and fathers, we are called upon to learn from, respond to, and follow our heavenly Father's established pattern of initiation.

BIG BOY GOSPEL: UNDERSTANDING YOUR BIBLICAL RESPONSIBILITY

How do we as husbands and fathers set the tone in our household? It begins by first taking ownership and understanding that it is our biblical responsibility to set the tone in our homes and thus in our families in the first place. As husbands and fathers, we need to do what Adam refused to do in the Garden. Adam refused to take responsibility for the moral-spiritual condition of his family. When God came looking for Adam in the Garden to give account for the actions of his family, instead of him taking the blame, he shifted the blame to his wife. In other words, Adam initiated a pattern of blame shifting or passing the buck. Eve responded to Adam's initiation and lack of leadership by doing the same thing. Adam blamed Eve for the sin of the family, and Eve, in turn, blamed the serpent (Genesis 3:13). As husbands and fathers we need to understand that the buck begins and ends with us. We need to understand that with position and authority comes responsibility.

Most husbands, whether they've gone to church their entire life, or have never set foot in a church building, know at least one verse in the Bible that they are quick to sling at their wives when they feel that they are out of order: "For the husband is the head of the wife…"(Ephesians 5:23). We can't claim to be the *man* and the *head* of our family simply in title; we must also be willing to take the responsibility that comes with the title. This may be hard for some men reading this book to swallow, but if our houses are out of order and all hell is breaking loose, it is our fault. If our wives are habitually disrespectful and rebellious, we need to ask ourselves in what ways have we neglected our biblical responsibility to show them unconditional love? Do we constantly criticize our wives and tear them down with our words or actions? Likewise, if our children are unruly and refuse to honor their mother, we need to ask ourselves, how have we failed as leaders of our family? How have our children followed our mistakes and poor examples? Have we freely dishonored or disrespected our children's mother in front of them? Are we frequently emotionally and spiritually unavailable to our children? If our home life or marriage is in shambles we have to take responsibility. We cannot blame our wives. We cannot blame our children. We must take full responsibility and take the blame. As psychologist and Christian author, Dr. James Dobson, points out in his book titled *Straight Talk to Men and Their Wives*:

A Christian man is obligated to lead his family to the best of his ability…If his family has purchased too many items on credit, then the financial crunch is ultimately his fault. If the family never reads the Bible or seldom goes to church on Sunday, God holds the man to blame. If the children are disrespectful and disobedient, the primary responsibility lies with the father…not his wife…In my view, America's greatest need is for husbands to begin guiding their families, rather than pouring every physical and emotional resource into the mere acquisition of money (p. 64).[1]

Taking responsibility for the moral-spiritual health of our family is part of our job description as husbands and fathers. My brother, this book will not help you grow if everything I write is easy to digest and apply in your life. The Apostle Paul made a distinction in 1 Corinthians 3:2 that some parts of the Gospel are much more easier to digest than others. In his analogy, "milk" represented the basics of the faith. Meat, on the other hand, represents the parts of God's Word that are much more difficult to digest, but are very crucial for our spiritual growth. This is the big boy gospel. If you want to set the tone in your household as "the man" and leader of your family, you have to learn to form your lips and say: "I am the captain of this ship, and if the ship goes down... I am responsible, I am accountable, it is my fault.

TAKING THE BULL BY THE HORNS: EMBRACING YOUR BIBLICAL RESPONSIBILITY TO LEAD

If we genuinely desire healthy marriages and emotionally and spiritually healthy children, we have to take the bull by the horns and properly lead by example. It is incumbent upon husbands and fathers to initiate and see to it that their family prays together and that they understand that honoring God and attending weekly church services as a family unit are priorities. Ultimately, it is the father's responsibility to ensure that his children understand the moral standards and values of the family and that respecting their mother and other authority figures isn't an option, it is a requirement.

Furthermore, it is the husband's responsibility to communicate and see to it that the family understands that the Word of God is the foundation or basis of everything the family values and the reason why the family functions in the way that it does. In short, one of the most important responsibilities of husbands and fathers is to make sure that their wives and children comprehend the vision and direction of the family, and that they understand their role and function in the Kingdom.

To be clear, I am not suggesting that husbands and fathers need to do all the thinking, planning, and initiating in the family. Rather, they need to demonstrate a general pattern of initiation and take primary responsibility for the moral-spiritual life of the family. As John Piper so eloquently states:

> There will be many times and many areas of daily life where the wife will do all kinds of planning and initiating. But there is a general tone and pattern of initiative that should develop which is sustained by the husband. For example, the leadership pattern would be less than Biblical if the wife in general was having to take initiative in prayer at mealtime, and get the family out of bed for worship on

Sunday morning, and gather the family for devotions, and discuss what moral standards will be required of the children... [or] confer about financial priorities...a wife may initiate the discussion and planning of any one of these but if she becomes the one who senses the general responsibility for this pattern of initiative while her husband is passive, something contrary to Biblical masculinity and femininity is in the offing (p. 39).[2]

Adam chose not to say anything and be passive as Eve ate from the tree of knowledge of good and evil and gave the fruit to him to eat also. As husbands, we cannot be passive and watch our wives take primary responsibility for the direction and decision making of our families. It is incumbent upon us to be vocal in what we say and what we do and intentional in our leadership. We must lead by example and initiation, being mindful that our wives and children are watching and potentially following the example we set. It's not good enough to tell our wives and children that it is important to go to church, pray or do devotion; we have to show them how it should be done. They should be able to see the way we live and follow our example. Of course, it goes without saying that our lives need to line up with the Word of God, and we have to be present in their lives emotionally and physically if we expect our wives and children to properly respond to our initiation.

WHEN YOU FALL, GET BACK UP!

The great inventor, Thomas Edison, said: "Our greatest weakness lies in giving up…the most certain way to succeed is always to try just one more time." I cannot guarantee that this journey will be easy. I cannot promise that you will never miss the mark as a husband or father again. Falling will most likely be a part of your journey to becoming a better spouse to your wife or father to your children. The issue isn't if you fall…because you most certainly will; but rather, when you fall, how will you respond? Even great leaders fall sometimes. In our own personal paths to be successful husbands and fathers, Edison encourages us with these words: "…the most certain way to succeed is always to try just one more time."

If we abort the process of becoming God's man, we will forfeit all that God has for us and disqualify ourselves from the opportunity to see our families and marriages blessed. This isn't an easy process, but if you continue to try, just one more time, eventually you will arrive at your desired destination as a competent and effective leader of your home. Great success seldom occurs without great failure or struggle. Just ask great leaders like Steve Jobs, Mahatma Gandhi, Abraham Lincoln, or Michael Jordan.

Before Steve Jobs became the tech visionary of our

generation, he was unceremoniously forced out of Apple in 1985, less than a decade after he built and co-founded the company. A demoralizing moment in his life, Jobs called his firing "a devastating...and very public failure."[3] Likewise, Gandhi's road to success also started off quite bumpy. After law school, he tried and failed twice to establish himself as a lawyer in India. Gandhi lacked the basic skills to properly cross-examine witnesses. Embarrassed and devastated, Gandhi never practiced law in a courtroom again. Similarly, Abraham Lincoln was no stranger to failure. Before he became one of the greatest presidents of the United States, Lincoln failed in business, was defeated for state legislature, and after finally being elected to the U.S. Congress in 1846, lost re-election two years later. In fact, in the six years prior to Lincoln's presidential election, he was defeated as a vice presidential nominee, and twice lost a bid for the U.S. Senate. Finally, prior to Jordan winning his first three NBA Championships, he spent three consecutive seasons being eliminated in the playoffs by his Eastern Conference rivals—the Detroit Pistons. It wasn't until their fourth consecutive meeting in the playoffs (1991 Eastern Conference Finals), that Michael Jordan and the Bulls finally beat the Pistons, moving on to win his first of six NBA Championships. These stories should be a reminder that great leaders often develop in the context of great trials, great struggles and great lows.

Imagine for a moment, if Steve Jobs gave up and stopped sharpening his skills as an innovator after his firing in 1985. Consider had Ghandi succeeded as a lawyer, would he have ever turned his attention elsewhere, and developed a passion for civil rights? What if President Lincoln would have given up prematurely? Would history have turned out dramatically different? Finally, imagine if Michael Jordan left the Chicago Bulls after his first six seasons of his career and decided to "take his talents" to an aging Pistons team, would he go down in history as the greatest player to lead a team to an NBA championship or would he be considered a good basketball player that never reached his full potential? At the end of the day, thank God these great leaders did not quit. Each made a decision in spite of failure, disappointment, or embarrassment, to dust themselves off, and try just one more time. If they had given up prematurely, they would have forfeited the opportunity to leave behind a great legacy.

Maybe you've fallen. You may have made mistakes. Perhaps you've neglected your wife or been emotionally unavailable and disconnected to your children. You need to know that there is hope, and if you want to recover, you can't stay down for the count, you must dust yourself off, get up, and continue to try just one more time.

THE MILLION-DOLLAR QUESTION

The million-dollar question each of us needs to answer as husbands and fathers is: what is the example that we are currently setting in our homes and families? Are we leaders worth following, or are we setting the wrong example? Are we being passive in our leadership, or are we taking the initiative and establishing ourselves in our households as husbands and fathers who display a general pattern of unconditional love, support, protection, and provision for our families? Wherever we are and however we've failed in the past, it's important that we first acknowledge that if our family is to get back on track it's our responsibility, not our wives, not our children or anyone else for that matter.

Second, we have to acknowledge how we've missed the mark, repent, and ask the Lord to renew our minds so that we can conform to His image and become the husbands and fathers that we are called to be (Romans 12:2). Third, we have to follow God's blueprint for biblical manhood outlined in His Word. Finally, we need to understand that family restoration is a process and it often takes time. We need to be committed to the process and apply biblical principles in our marriages and relationships with our children. In other words, we need to recognize that the condition of our families did not unravel in a few days, so we shouldn't expect everything to improve in a few days either. Time does not heal all wounds; God heals wounds. Sometimes it takes time to rebuild what took months or years to tear down. We have to be patient, stay the course, and look to God to be our help.

Footnotes

1 Dobson, James. *Straight Talk to Men and Their Wives.* Waco, Texas: Words Books. 1980

2 Piper, John. "A Vision of Biblical Complementarity." *Recovering Biblical Manhood and Womanhood: A Response to Evangelical Feminism.* Ed. John Piper and Wayne Grudem. Wheaton, Illinois: Crossway, 2006 (Second Edition). 31-59.

3 Siegel, Joel. "When Jobs Got Fired By Apple." *ABC News.* 6 October. 2011. Web.

PART III

Husbands and Fathers as Providers of Their Households

My father grew up in an era when being a good father meant providing for one's wife and children financially. My father had a great work ethic. He worked long hours and made sure that we had a roof over our heads, clothes on our backs, and food in our stomachs. I honor my father for the sacrifices he made, and the great lengths he took to provide for our family. In fact, as I watched him through the years, I too learned, that a central component of manhood, and thus fatherhood, was providing financial security for one's family.

Although my father shared his financial resources with us, I can honestly say that I barely knew my father as a person. We had very few conversations and he rarely gave me advice or guidance. I couldn't fully articulate it at the time, but I knew something was wrong, that *something* was off or missing. The absence of his emotional-spiritual presence and lack of physical engagement in my life left a void. I longed for an intimate relationship with my father. I longed to know who he was as a person; I deeply desired to know his story. I longed to understand what moved him, what motivated him, as well as his strengths, weaknesses, and fears. I longed for his involvement in my life. Due to my father's emotional unavailability, I struggled with who I was as a person and as a young man.

THE BEST GAME OF MY LIFE

I played little league baseball throughout my adolescence. In my mind, I was a pretty decent player. I wasn't an all-star by any means, but I could hold my own with other kids my age. With the exception of one baseball game, my father never came to any of my games. For the one game my father made, I recall looking up and seeing my father sitting in the bleachers with a friend he brought with him.

It was in that game that I remember playing the best little league game of my life. I ran like I never ran and I hit the ball like I never hit the ball before. I found myself more focused and driven in that game than I have ever been. I had made up my mind that day that I was not going to look bad in front of my father. I wanted to impress my dad. I wanted my dad to be proud of his son; I wanted my father's approval more than anything else. This game stands out more than any game in my mind because it represented a moment in my life where I felt an emotional connection with my dad and I sensed his love and support. My dad took the time and made an effort to support me with his presence. On that day, my dad decided to invest in me as a person. It was in this moment that I felt most connected to my father as his son. Because he decided to show up, the game took on special significance. As my father's son, I wanted to do well, and make my father proud. It was in this game, that I felt emotionally secure. I felt secure in who I was as a young boy and in my identity as my father's son. In this one game, I went from an average player to a great player in a matter of minutes. I literally felt like superman on the day my father showed up to my baseball game for the first time. I'm convinced that if a wall was in front of me, I would have run right through it. My father's engagement and active involvement in that moment of my life made all the difference.

I learned an important lesson that day that sticks with me as a father today: When fathers are intimately involved and engaged, it has an empowering and energizing impact on the lives of their children to do their very best and be their very best. For me, this life lesson translated into my relationship with my son, MJ. I am committed to being there for my son. I am committed to letting him know that Daddy loves him and that his father is proud of him. When I greet MJ after school or go out of town, I make a point to let my son know that I missed him. Even when I am busy studying, paying bills, or watching a football game (and I love my football), if MJ approaches me for my attention or affection I make a point to stop what I am doing to give him my undivided attention. It is important to me that I make myself available to him; that he senses that his father is available and accessible if he needs me.

I spent many years feeling like my father was unavailable and inaccessible. I loved my dad, but I often felt like I had to walk on eggshells when I was around him. At times, I felt emotionally insecure, and on many occasions, I questioned whether my father ever loved me. I did not want that for my son. Although MJ is nonverbal, I can see in his eyes the energizing effect of giving him my time, physical touch, and conversation. He doesn't have to guess whether I love him or not, I can see the security and joy he has while in my presence. I can sense that MJ knows that he is loved and is secure in the love that he receives from me. MJ has what I did not have growing up, and it makes a world of difference in his life.

OUR BIBLICAL RESPONSIBILITY: PROVIDERS OF THE HOME

As husbands and fathers, we frequently spend a lot of time, energy, and attention on our jobs or careers, hobbies, personal ambitions, and even ministry, while our family life either suffers or falls completely by the wayside. Corporate and political legacies or legacies in sports and entertainment should never be the ultimate life aim or purpose of husbands and fathers. The most important legacy or impact that we can make on this world is that which we can leave to our wives, sons, and daughters. Don't take my word for it; take God's Word for it. First Timothy 5:8 (NASB) states: "But if anyone does not provide [care for, look after] for his own, and especially for those of his [own] household, he has denied the faith and is worse than an unbeliever." In this verse, Paul likens the neglect of one's family as being worse than an unbeliever. In other words, it is our duty and responsibility as men to first care for and look after the needs of our family members, in general, but we have a special obligation to care for those who reside in our own household. To neglect this Christian duty and responsibility is essentially worse than refusing to believe in Christ in the first place.

Mature men are providers for their wives and children. To provide for one's family is to meet their needs. This may seem obvious, but in reality as husbands and fathers we often attempt to meet the material or physical needs of our family, while overlooking their spiritual, emotional, or social needs. Adam made this mistake in the third chapter of Genesis. After the fall, the Bible states: "...Then the eyes of both of them were opened, and they knew that they were naked; and they sewed fig leaves together and made loin coverings" (Genesis 3:7, NASB). In other words, after the Fall, Adam focused on the task of sewing together fig leaves to cover his newly discovered nakedness.

Like many men today, Adam's focus was on covering his family's immediate physical need (nakedness), while overlooking the more weighty spiritual consequence of their sin. Before we judge Adam, we often find ourselves in the same predicament. We compensate for our lack of involvement and engagement in the lives of our wives and children with new cars, new clothes and the latest iPhone or television. We think that we fulfill our role as fathers saying, "I go to work and put food on the table," but at the end of the day our children are crying for our time and are desperate for our physical presence.

Providing for our families is more than bringing financial resources to the table. We provide for our wives and children by giving of ourselves—by giving our wives and children our time. We also give of ourselves through our involvement and engagement in the lives of our wives and children and the extent to which we meet their spiritual, emotional, and social needs. As a husband and father who also happens to be a pastor, one of my most important priorities is to ensure that my family is spiritually aligned to the will of God. One of the things I established early in my marriage was to set times for my family to pray together so that we have opportunities to connect and develop spiritual intimacy with God and with one another. My wife followed the pattern of initiation that I set, and prays with and covers our son in prayer each morning before she drops him off at school. I also initiate times of family retreat. I initiate several minor family getaways throughout the year and I make sure my wife and I have at least three or four extended vacations each year.

As a pastor of a rapidly growing church with over 7,000 members and various national obligations and responsibilities, I am extremely busy. I have to be intentional with my time and make a point to communicate to my wife and son that it's important that they understand that family is valued and that setting aside family time and opportunities to rest and regroup is vital to the welfare of our family. Outside of my relationship with God, my wife and child are the most important persons in my life.

You will see in the next three chapters, the various ways in which God provided for Adam and Eve after Creation, and what we can learn from the pattern of provision that God set. I then transition to the responsibility of men as providers today and the threefold benefits of biblical provision (financial security, emotional security and spiritual security).

CHAPTER 8 ——————

Providing God's Way

Throughout Scripture, God is presented to us as a provider. After the Lord supplied Abraham with a ram as a burnt offering to take the place of his son, Isaac, Abraham called Mount Moriah the place where "The Lord Will Provide" (Genesis 22:13-14). In the book of Daniel, God provided for the three Hebrew boys, Shadrach, Meshach, and Abednego, delivering them from a fiery furnace (Daniel 3:16-17). Throughout the gospels, God showed Himself as a provider, supplying our most pressing need by sacrificing His Son for the atonement of our sin (Romans 3:25). God continues to show Himself as a provider to believers, today, by promising to meet all of our needs by Christ Jesus (Philippians 4:19).

GOD'S PROVISION IN CREATION

God's personality as a provider can also be clearly seen in the creation narrative. After Creation, God provided for mankind in at least three ways: First, God provided for Adam by creating a physical space where he could share of his substance (*financial/ material security*). In other words, God took care of Adam's most basic needs for food and shelter, placing him in an environment where he was surrounded by every material and natural resource that he needed to thrive. Second, God supplied Adam with a home. By home I mean a safe and secure environment that he could call his own (*emotional security*). Finally, God provided for Adam by giving him the greatest possible resource—Himself (*spiritual security*). That is, God developed a relationship with Adam and was intimately connected, involved, and engaged in every aspect of his life. In this way, God gave Adam (and later Eve) the gift of security. Adam was secure in God's provision. He was secure in knowing that God would meet his most basic needs. Adam was also emotionally secure in that Eden was a safe and secure environment that he could call his own. Finally, Adam was spiritually secure in his personal relationship with God, and in turn, was emotionally secure in who he was (his identity) and what he was called to do (his purpose and destiny).

GOD'S PROVISION FOR ADAM: ALL OF ADAM'S BASIC NEEDS WERE MET

God gave Adam financial and material security by first sharing of His substance. God placed Adam in a physical space or environment where all of his basic needs for food and shelter were fully met. In other words, Adam had all of the food and natural resources he needed. It was in the context of this resource-rich environment, that God gave Adam the best possible opportunity to thrive. Genesis 2:9a points out that God caused every tree to grow in the Garden that was both "pleasing to the sight" and "good for food." Furthermore, the tree of life was in the middle of the Garden, giving Adam the opportunity to live in perfect health forever (Genesis 2:9b). We later learn that a river flowed out of Eden to water the Garden (Genesis 2:10). Eden was surrounded by rich land and natural resources like gold and onyx. By placing Adam in a resource-rich environment, God provided for Adam (and Eve's) present needs, but He also laid a sound foundation for their family to thrive for future generations.

GOD'S PROVISION FOR ADAM: THE GIFT OF EMOTIONAL SECURITY

God also gave Adam the gift of emotional security. God established a safe and secure atmosphere (or home) for Adam, placing Adam in an environment that was specifically designed with his needs and interest in mind. In fact, everything that God created was established and designed with Adam in mind. The Garden was created for Adam, for his comfort, enjoyment, and use. We often misread the second chapter of Genesis and gloss over the fact that the Garden was created *after* Adam was formed from the dust of the earth. The Garden wasn't formed … and then mankind was an afterthought. Genesis 2:8 states: "And the Lord God planted a garden eastward in Eden; and there he put the man he had formed" (KJV). In other words, the Garden was created and designed with the intention of providing an environment that perfectly suited Adam's need to have a place or space that he could call his own.

It's important to note that God did more than simply create a space for Adam to live (a house). God did much more than that. God created an environment for Adam and his future family to thrive (a home). God went to great lengths to affirm to Adam that the Garden was made for him. First, Adam was told that it was his responsibility to tend to and guard or oversee the Garden (Genesis 2:15). Second, God communicated to Adam that he could freely eat from any tree in the Garden except the tree of the knowledge of good and evil (Genesis 2:16-17). Third, God empowered Adam to name every animal on the face of the earth (Genesis 2:19), and finally, God communicated to Adam and Eve that they were destined to have dominion or rulership on the earth (Genesis 1:28).

In the second chapter of Genesis, God is presented to us as a master architect and city planner. The Garden was a perfect environment. God provided an environment for Adam that was safe and secure, an environment that was designed with him in mind, a place that Adam could call his home. It's clear that through God's provision, He was setting the tone of His relationship with mankind and an environment that would lay the foundation for healthy family relationships. God didn't force Adam to love Him or respect Him, but rather through His provision initiated a general pattern of unconditional love and support for His creation. Adam and Eve properly responded to the environment that God established. By Genesis 2:25 the Bible says: "…And the man and his wife were both naked and unashamed." In other words, Adam and Eve had nothing to hide; they felt completely secure and emotionally vulnerable with one another and with God. This wasn't by accident, but was the direct result of the atmosphere that God created in Eden and the pattern of loving initiation that He set.

GOD'S PROVISION FOR ADAM: THE BENEFITS OF A RELATIONSHIP WITH GOD

In addition to providing for Adam's most basic needs of food and shelter, and creating a safe and secure environment where Adam and his future family could flourish and feel safe and secure, God gave Adam the greatest resource: Himself. By giving of Himself, God developed a relationship with Adam sharing His time, wisdom and direction. It is in this context that God gave Adam an identity, telling him who he was, and what he was capable of. In particular, God gave Adam an assignment and a job to do. Adam's divine assignment was to "cultivate" or "keep/guard" the Garden and to take up the leadership position in the family (Genesis 2:15). As the "master landscaper" of the Garden, God empowered Adam with the ability to provide for his family's material needs (food) by using his hands in labor. God also gave Adam direction and clear boundaries on how he desired for him to live and prosper, telling him which trees he could and could not freely eat from, and how he should conduct himself as the federal head of all mankind (Genesis 2:16-17; Romans 5:12). God gave Adam a companion and suitable helper (Eve) to assist him in accomplishing his God-given assignment (Genesis 2:18). Finally, after Eve comes on the scene, God speaks into and over Adam's and Eve's lives by blessing them both and commanding them to be fruitful and multiply (Genesis 1:28). It is through God's involvement and engagement in Adam's and Eve's lives that He affirms them by telling them that they have the power and authority to rule. God shows Himself strong as a provider by letting Adam and Eve know that everything that He created on the earth, He did with them in mind with the specific purpose of supplying them with food and shelter, and providing them the opportunity to take delight in and enjoy that which was at their fingertips (Genesis 1:29; Genesis 2:9).

God wasn't just a provider in that He gave Adam a place he could call home and shared His substance with him; He was also a provider in that He was intimately involved in and engaged in Adam's life. It's clear in Scripture that Adam and Eve *knew* God on an intimate level. They knew and understood what God thought about them and who He called them to be. God shared His time with them, He shared His wisdom with them, and He gave them purpose and divine assignments. Mature husbands and fathers follow God's lead.

CHAPTER 9 —————

Man and His Family: Providing Financial Security

If you ask the average man what it means to provide for his family, he will more than likely talk about the importance of meeting one's family's basic financial and material needs. Similar to my dad, men today, would most likely define their role as providers by focusing on the importance of keeping a roof over their family's head, making sure their wife and children have clothes to wear, and seeing to it that everyone has food to eat.

Although financial provision is a very important dimension of caring for one's family (and one dimension that many brothers have failed to provide), it only represents a single dimension of provision from a biblical perspective. Providing is more than simply meeting one's family's physical and material needs. Mature fathering and husbanding is multidimensional. Biblically mature men provide by giving their wives and children what they need the most: financial security, emotional security, and spiritual security. Our families feel financially secure when they have a sense that their basic financial and material need for food, shelter, and clothing will be met. Our wives and children gain emotional security when they sense that we are committed to loving and caring for them with our words and actions, and through our intimate involvement and engagement in their lives. Finally, mature men provide spiritual security for their family as they demonstrate a personal conviction that God is the ultimate source of provision, and it is in Him, all of our needs as a family are met.

MATURE HUSBANDS AND FATHERS PROVIDE FINANCIAL SECURITY

Mature men provide for their families by first giving them financial security. By financial security, I am referring to giving our wives and children a sense that we will meet their most basic need for food, shelter, and clothing. One of the first things that God did after He placed Adam in the Garden is He gave Adam a job—an assignment (Genesis 2:15). I believe God was making an important statement when He did this. He was demonstrating that even when a man has every possible resource at his disposal (potential), he cannot truly thrive outside of his purpose and work. God gave Adam the responsibility to "cultivate" and "keep" the Garden (Genesis 2:15). In cultivating and keeping the Garden, God was giving Adam more than just a job; He was giving him the means by which he could provide for the basic needs of his future family. By "working" the Garden he was given the ability to feed his family.

Any man who is worth his salt wants to work and share what he's earned with those he loves. Work is part of the DNA of a man. Biblically mature men desire to work, and view their work or labor as an important part of their identity and an opportunity to provide for the needs of their family. This is why if you find a man who is out of work he is normally miserable. Men who do not sense a responsibility to work and or provide for their family have a distorted sense of masculinity, and thus, their manhood. This includes men who have little desire to work, able-bodied men who have no problem allowing the women in their lives to take care of them financially, or men who work but squander earnings designated for their family on things like gambling, alcohol, drugs, or other addictions. When we find a man who does not want to work or who refuses to provide for his family, he is operating in dysfunction and is functioning outside of the specific purpose in which he was designed for as a man.

I often tell the single women in my congregation that it doesn't matter how good a man looks if he isn't working. There cannot be romance without finance. When you come home and the lights are shut off because the electric company turned them off for non-payment, I promise you the mood that will be set on that evening will not be romance. It is important for me to add, however, that I am very aware that there are many men who desire to work but do not have employment due to sickness, lay-offs, and the high unemployment rate that we face. The women in their lives should always seek to encourage them during this period since their sense of manhood is challenged during this time.

ARE TRADITIONAL WORK/FAMILY ROLES OBSOLETE IN THE 21ST CENTURY?

I know we live in a time of women's liberation. We live in a time where women as a group have experienced growing educational and occupational opportunities since the 1970s. I am also aware of the common societal belief that as long as someone in the family has a job or is gainfully employed, it's okay for wives to work outside the home and husbands to stay at home. The Bible suggests otherwise. Such an arrangement does not fit the Old Testament (Genesis 2:15-16) or New Testament descriptions of mature manhood and thus, one's masculinity (2 Thessalonians 3:10; 1 Timothy 5:8; Ephesians 5:23; 1 Corinthians 11:3). God's original plan and design for male-female relations were that men take the lead in working outside the home and bring financial and material resources into the home, while it was the responsibility of women to take the lead in the domain of the home. Household arrangements that follow a different pattern reflect a role reversal of God's original design.

MARRIED COUPLES AND THE DIVISION OF LABOR

This does not mean in the case of married couples that wives cannot help in the pursuit of caring and providing for the basic needs of the family for food, shelter, and clothing. Nor does it mean that family financial planning should look more like a dictatorship rather than a partnership (which is unbiblical when we consider that men should be loving and compassionate servant-leaders). But rather it implies that men should take the primary leadership role in providing for the needs of the family.

I am aware that in many households both husbands and wives work. Furthermore, for many American households, wives earn more than their husbands. Does this mean that husbands who earn less than their wives are less than men, or are immature in their masculinity? Absolutely not. Being a mature man has less to do with how much money you earn, and more to do with an attitude, that is, a desire and posture to work or be gainfully employed. Mature men shouldn't simply have a job, they should feel compelled to work to the best of their God-given ability and potential to earn an honest wage and provide for the financial needs of their family. Biblically mature men feel it is their responsibility to provide for the financial and material needs of their family, and they understand that if God was to come looking for someone to give account for caring for the most basic needs of the family, He would come looking for the husband first. As the well known pastor and author John Piper states:

When there is no bread on the table it is the man that should feel the main pressure to do something to get it there...man will [or at least should] feel his personhood compromised, if he through sloth [laziness] or folly or lack of discipline, becomes dependent over the long haul on his wife's income (p. 42).[1]

As highlighted in earlier chapters, it's important that husbands and fathers understand that it is their biblical responsibility to care for the welfare of their family. Financial provision is no different. Men should sense or feel a responsibility to provide for the financial and material needs of their wives and children.

FINANCIAL AND FAMILY PLANNING

In the case of more practical financial needs like budgeting, this doesn't necessarily mean that husbands need to be over the day-to-day budgeting or record keeping of the finances, but rather it is their primary responsibility to see to it that the family does have a working budget, the family is actively planning and setting goals for their financial future, and if the family has debt, they are working together to actively pay it off. The point isn't so much who does the budget as long as the husband takes on the responsibility to see to it that it is done.

Marriage is about finding out what your strengths and weaknesses are, and not being afraid of encouraging your wife to use her strengths for the good of the household. Brothers, if you know that you are a poor budgeter, and your wife, on the other hand, meticulously writes down everything she spends, then by all means give her the authority to manage the family's finances. If your wife manages the finances because that's her area of strength and your area of weakness, it does not make you any less a man. In fact, it is the exact opposite: such a household decision makes you a very wise man.

It goes without saying that husbands should both value and listen to their wives' potential contribution to family planning, in general, and financial planning, in particular, before decisions are made. But the final decision-making and the main pressure of meeting the needs of the family should fall on the shoulders of men. As King Solomon points out, when we have a godly and virtuous wife, our heart should trust or have full confidence in her (Proverbs 31:11). This means that we should value our wives' thoughts, opinions, and intuition, and be careful about making unilateral decisions that may affect our household. Every good man needs a good wife. Good wives add value and favor to their husband's lives (Proverbs 18:22).

NONRESIDENTIAL FATHERS AND THEIR CHILDREN

Many fathers today, due to never marrying their children's mother, divorce, separation, or remarriage, find themselves living in different households from their children. Even under these circumstances, mature fathers should sense the weight of responsibility to see to it that they meet the financial needs of their children. They should sense this financial responsibility and obligation whether they are still dating or are on good terms with the mother of their children or not. Fathers, who do not sense this responsibility, have a distorted sense of manhood, and have yet to mature as a man. The federal government shouldn't have to tell you that you should pay child support, buy clothes/diapers for your children and make sure they have a roof over their heads or food in the house where they reside. It is your responsibility to see to it that your children's needs are met. Even if it's the case that the mother or mothers of your children marry or re-marry, her union with another man does not absolve you of your responsibility to look after and care for the financial and material needs of your children.

HEALTHY FATHERING VS. SPOILING CHILDREN

Providing for your children doesn't look like giving your children everything they want or spoiling your children. Immature fathers (and mothers for that matter) often give their children everything they want because they didn't have those things themselves as a child or because they are more intent on pleasing their child and being their friend than being their parent. Such behaviors often lead to children who are not ready for the reality of the world and who develop attitudes of entitlement and ungratefulness. Instead, mature fathers give their children what they need: a place to stay, food to eat, and clothes to wear. Children who are given such things are ready to face the real world and often become emotionally and spiritually healthy adults. Although my father wasn't perfect, he made sure that my family had the basics. I was financially secure and my basic needs were met. Other children I grew up around who didn't have their financial needs met, attempted to meet their own need for food and clothing through illegal means. They felt that it was necessary to steal to survive or get by. Although some of my friends encouraged me to do so, I never felt the need to shoplift clothes from the mall, to grab women's purses in the park, or to steal food from the local grocery store.

Children, and it's certainly the case for wives too, who have their financial and material needs met at home, have no need to look outside of the home to make up the difference. Mature husbands and fathers make it their responsibility to see to it that the financial and material needs of their family are met, and that their wives and children have a sense of financial security.

CHAPTER 10 —————

Man and His Family: Providing Emotional Security

Our wives and children also need to feel emotionally secure. Emotional security is a gift that our wives and children gain when they sense that we are committed to loving and caring for them with our words and actions, and through our intimate involvement and engagement in their lives. Emotional security begins with the environment that we establish in our home, and the pattern of initiation that we set for our family.

Mature, Godly men give the gift of emotional security to their families by first making it a priority to give their families a safe and secure space that they can call their own (a home). Similar to how God prepared a home for Adam and surrounded him with every resource one would need to be successful, we have to prepare an environment for our wives and children that would put them in the best possible position to thrive.

Don't miss this point. I am not saying that mature men need to purchase a *house* for their wives and children to live. Wives and children need more than a physical space to thrive; they need a *home*. That is, they need a place or space to live that is safe and secure, and an environment that is uniquely their own. A house is a physical edifice that often provides financial and material security; but a home provides emotional security, and lays the foundation for healthy social-emotional-spiritual family relationships to flourish.

Adam was being prophetic when he said, "...for this reason a man should leave his father and mother, and be joined to his wife" (Genesis 2:24). Leaving is indicative of removing one's self from the place or environment that one's parent(s) established, and carving out a space or place of your own. Brothers, it doesn't matter if the home that you establish is 500 square feet or 5000 square feet as long as the atmosphere you set is one that makes your wife and children emotionally safe and secure.

God set the tone of the environment in Eden and He empowered Adam to set the tone of his relationship with Eve (Genesis 2:24-25). Like Adam, mature husbands and fathers properly respond to the God-given calling on their lives by making it a priority to establish a distinct space or environment that their wives and children can call home. Providing a "home" for one's family is essential for laying the foundation for healthy interpersonal, family, and spiritual relationships.

A WORD TO SINGLE MEN

I believe this also applies to single, engaged and pre-engaged men as well. Again Adam is our perfect model for how a single man ought to prepare to be a husband in the future. Immediately after Creation, Adam was single or unmarried in the sense that he did not have a female companion. Before Eve came on the scene God prepared Adam for his future wife (and family) by ensuring that he had a job/assignment (Genesis 2:15), that he understood God's law (Genesis 2:16-17), that he had a personal relationship with God (Genesis 2:18-22), and finally, that he understood that the nature of marital relationships is to leave one's family's home in a physical and spiritual sense and establish their own (Genesis 2:23-25).

In other words, Adam both understood and prophesied that before a man becomes married he is called to *leave* the place or space that his parents established and *cleave* or *prepare* a new home for his wife and (future) children. It was in this new environment that God ordained that husband and wife have the opportunity to build a new life together, and lay the foundation for healthy family relationships. This isn't simply a nice speech that Adam makes or an idealized fairy tale; this is a spiritual mandate from God and the precise model that we should follow as men. If we are to properly respond to this divine mandate to leave and cleave (Genesis 2:24), before we marry it is critical that we first establish a place or space separate or distinct from our parents and family. It is in this space that we need to learn who we are as men. A space where we can develop a personal relationship with God, get in tune with the gifts and talents we have inside of us, and prayerfully discover what God has placed us on this earth to do. This also looks like learning God's law (His Word) for ourselves and grappling with the wounds and scars of our past.

It is in the context of this space, that we learn to fear God, and begin to allow the Lord to do spiritual surgery on our hearts and minds, conforming to His perfect image and will (Romans 8:29; Philippians 2:5). Transformed, healed, and renewed from the inside out, this is the process by which we graduate from being boys and transition to becoming men. This process is a critical one. A man cannot give his wife and children the gift of emotional security if he doesn't have it himself.

The point of this isn't to discourage married men who are still grappling with their past, developing a relationship with God, or becoming emotionally secure in who they are as men. Unmarried and broken or married and struggling, God is our help no matter where we are in the process—even if we messed up, our home environment is in shambles, or it seems like our family is quickly sinking like the Titanic. It is not too late to turn our house into a home and begin the process of giving our wife and children the gift of emotional security. It may take time, but I am a living witness that God is faithful! Like Adam, mature husbands and fathers and future husbands and fathers, properly respond to the God-given calling on their lives by establishing a distinct space or place that their wives and children can call home. Providing a "home" for one's family is essential for laying the foundation for healthy interpersonal, family, and spiritual relationships.

RESPONDING PROPERLY TO GOD'S MANDATE FOR HEALTHY FAMILY RELATIONSHIPS

It's important that we know our wife and children personally and intimately and that they know us.

Before the fall, Adam was in perfect spiritual alignment with His Creator, and his marriage could best be characterized by unity, intimacy, transparency, and trust: "And Adam said...[man shall]...leave his father and mother, and shall cleave unto his wife: and they shall be one flesh. And they were both naked, the man and his wife, and were not ashamed" (Genesis 2:23-25). Notice that Adam wasn't cut off emotionally from his wife, but rather, he was emotionally involved and engaged in the relationship. He was naked and unashamed before her. He was transparent and vulnerable with her, and had nothing to hide. Eve properly responded to her husband's pattern of initiation as a provider. Adam made Eve feel emotionally secure; in turn, they were both naked and unashamed before one another and God. God desires husbands and wives to be connected to one another in a very deep and intimate way. God's intent was that husband and wife become "one flesh" (Genesis 2:24). Becoming one flesh is a profound spiritual process that if done properly requires us as husbands to be intimately involved and emotionally engaged in the lives of our wives.

BEING INTENTIONAL ABOUT YOUR EMOTIONAL PRESENCE

Being a real man means I am willing to invest in my

family. I'm not afraid to vocalize that I love them. I make a point to be physically and emotionally present and available in the highest moments of my family's life whether it's a championship game, a spelling bee, or a dance recital. But I am also present for my family during their lowest moments. Whether those low moments are when my child scrapes her knee after trying to ride a bike for the first time, when my pre-teen comes home crying because he failed a test, or (God forbid) my teenage son and/or daughter experiences a tough break-up with his or her high school sweetheart. The point is, we properly fulfill the biblical mandate to be fruitful and multiply (Genesis 1:28) when we play an active role in raising and rearing our children. Mature fathers make a point to be involved and engaged in their children's lives starting at conception and continuing throughout the duration of our lives.

It goes without saying, real and mature men aren't afraid to stick around when times are good and they have enough discernment to understand the necessity of their presence when times are difficult. Real men don't run and hide; they stand and fight for their families. When financial pressure or marital conflict occur in the home, biblically mature men don't run to the bar, lock themselves in a man cave, or play video games while shutting their family out.

Biblically mature men communicate through their words and actions that their family is a priority. They are committed to seeing to it that their presence is felt in their home, and intent on making a positive influence in the lives of their wives and children. Biblically mature men are also present and available physically, emotionally, socially, and spiritually. They make this statement through their actions: "Here are the most vulnerable parts of me. This is who I am. Learn from my mistakes. This is my story for better or worse."

In a practical sense, biblically mature men are willing to open up and be vulnerable with their family and allow them to know them beyond husband or father, but as a man too—a man who has the capacity to express emotion. A man who is multidimensional and complex experiencing a range of highs and lows such as fear, joy, sadness, excitement, loss, and gain.

It's important for your wife and children to know that you don't have all the answers and you aren't perfect, but you are striving to do the will of God. In so doing, you set a pattern of initiation that communicates to your family: "Here is all of me. I have nothing to hide." If you do this right and genuinely, your wives and children will feel emotionally secure, and will respond in kind: "Here is all of me. We have nothing to hide."

Our families so desperately need our presence and intimate engagement and involvement in their lives. It is not the case that all our wives need is to know that we will put food on the table and clothes on their backs. They also need to feel connected to us, not simply as fathers and husbands, but as a people and men.

EMOTIONAL SECURITY: RELIABILITY AND CONSISTENCY

Finally, biblically mature men give their families emotional security through their reliability and consistency as men. In other words, they have proved themselves as worthy leaders, men of integrity, and men of their word. It is quite difficult for children and wives to feel a sense of emotional security if their fathers and or husbands are constantly making poor choices and poor decisions. Likewise, men who are unreliable and rarely keep their word will also find difficulty ensuring that their children and wives experience emotional security. For many children, a string of broken promises will lead a child down the path of emotional insecurity. Similarly, wives feel emotionally insecure in their marriage when they don't feel or sense that their spouses love them or they sense that their marital relationship is on the rocks. Wives need to know that you are committed to the marriage, committed to working on the marriage, and growing as a husband and man.

Society views marriage as a social contract or commitment based on convenience that can be easily terminated by either party if things don't go their way. God views marriage as a covenant or life-long commitment based on unconditional love, loyalty, and devotion. A contract says we are committed to one another until we fall out of love. A covenant says that we are committed to one another for better or worse as long as we both shall live. Wives sense emotional security when they understand that whether our relationship is on cloud nine (for better) or it seems like we've hit rock bottom (for worse), we are committed to our marital union (covenant) for life.

The mistake that many husbands and wives make is, when their marriage appears to be at its worst and lowest moments they are quick to threaten their wives by bringing up divorce. Few things on this earth will sink your wife's heart and spiral her down the direction of emotional insecurity like using the "D-word" in a fight or argument. If we want to give our wives the gift of emotional security we need to establish that divorce is not an option. We need to establish that we are committed to our marriage for the rest of our lives, and that we are committed to growing as men and husbands for better or for worse.

If you've failed in any of these areas, you need to know that there is always hope for you. The remedy is to first repent to God and to your family. After you do this, make a commitment to your family to grow as a man, husband, and father. Finally, work towards providing the emotional security that your family so desperately needs through your intimate involvement and engagement in their life and by establishing a pattern of consistency and good decision-making. Biblically mature men are not perfect and are not too proud to say, 'I'm sorry,' and make things right. You'd be surprised at how far an apology goes to beginning the healing process for your wife or children. It may take time to restore your family's trust. It will take some time for your wife and children to feel emotionally secure. In the end, it will be well worth it!

There are benefits to giving our children and wives emotional security. When we give the gift of emotional security to our families, we witness and reap the blessing of healthy and happy relationships, children, and marriages.

THE BENEFITS OF EMOTIONAL SECURITY

Adam greatly benefited from God's intimate

involvement and engagement in his life. As a loving father, God gave Adam an identity telling him who he was and what he was called to do (Genesis 2:15). God also showed Adam what he was capable of (Genesis 2:19-20) and the authority he was given (Genesis 1:28). Finally, he blessed Adam and Eve (Genesis 1:28) while still giving them boundaries and clear expectations (Genesis 2:16).

As fathers, we are not God. But God graces us and gives us authority by virtue of our position of leadership in the family, to encourage our children and help them identify their God-given talents, to affirm that they are children of God and are destined for greatness, and to let them know that they are capable of doing great things and that they have authority in Christ that is without limits. As fathers, we also have the authority to speak blessings over and into the lives of our wives and children and to encourage our families to make God a priority in their life and to take their rightful place in the Kingdom of God.

Children who have fractured family relationships often have unhealthy family relationships as adults. They frequently have difficulty developing healthy friendships, struggle with trusting people, and frequently attract people who are broken and fractured like themselves. On the contrary, children who are healthy emotionally, socially, and spiritually grow up looking for healthy friendships, romantic relationships, and often develop a healthy relationship with God.

DISTORTED MASCULINITY: MEN AND THEIR EMOTIONS

Many men think that being a man means being self-reliant and not showing vulnerability or weakness, but this is not in line with God's original intent for the Adam of Creation and the Adams of today. Although such views of manhood are the norm in America today, they are contrary to biblical perspectives of healthy and mature manhood, and a distortion of God's original plan and design for man.

Being a man, in general, and husband and father, in particular, means that I am first and foremost, present. This isn't simply a physical presence in that we have a physical existence in the home, but rather, we have an emotional presence. Having an emotional presence in your home is a powerful statement to your family that you are committed to giving them emotional security, and that you are committed to being intimately involved and emotionally engaged in their lives. When we are involved and engaged, our children and wives feel emotionally secure. When we are absent altogether or present physically, but emotionally unavailable, our family feels abandoned.

For some, the terms 'men and emotions' go together just as well as oil and vinegar. The two almost seem to unnaturally mix, right? Here is my response: I am unfazed. Don't tell me that men are emotionless creatures and that it's easy (and perhaps natural) for women to emotionally engage and show passion. I don't even buy the excuse that men are emotionally deficient or that getting men to invest emotionally in anything is a near impossibility. I would go so far as to make the argument that men are some of the most emotional creatures that I know.

Have you been to a Super Bowl party lately? You know those parties where *unemotional* men wear football jerseys, yell at the television, and shout at the top of their lungs each time their favorite team makes a touchdown. How about the gym? Ever been there? You know, those places where *expressionless* men lift weights while moaning, groaning, and squealing, throwing weights on the ground and flexing for themselves in the mirror.

Men are indeed very emotional. We express a great deal of emotion about the things that we are passionate about. The question I want to ask you is: what are you passionate about? Is it a professional sport, your job or career, doing things outdoors like hunting or fishing, playing a team sport like bowling or baseball? Perhaps your thing is working out. Whatever your passion, I challenge you to make your family your passion and become intimately involved and emotionally engaged in the thing on this earth that we should love and care for the most—our families.

Whether we give our children financial security or emotional security, we have to learn that to be good husbands and fathers, we have to be and become whatever our children and wives need and be willing to make the adjustments to help meet their needs. When we have God in our lives, He will broaden our capacity to supply the needs of our wives and children as we mature in Him. This leads to the third and final dimension of biblical provision. As men we have limitations and it's important for us to recognize those limitations. It is in this context that our family needs more than financial, material, and emotional security; they need to feel spiritually secure. That is, they need to see that we have a genuine relationship with the Lord. They need to sense that we have a personal conviction that God is our ultimate source of provision, and it is in Him, that all of the family's needs shall be supplied.

Footnotes

1   Piper, John. "A Vision of Biblical Complementarity." *Recovering Biblical Manhood and Womanhood: A Response to Evangelical Feminism.* Ed. John Piper and Wayne Grudem. Wheaton, Illinois: Crossway, 2006 (Second Edition). 31-59.

CHAPTER 11 ———

Man and His God: Providing Spiritual Security for Your Family

When most men think of spirituality, they think of styles of praise and worship more commonly expressed by women. Many men think of crying, shouting, and the raising and lifting of one's hands as actions that only women do. Given that males are generally absent in many of the churches today, very few (if any) examples of male spirituality are present. Men frequently feel intimidated by stereotypically female spiritual expressions and thus struggle to express themselves in ways that make sense to men. Part of the problem is that many men grow up in homes where they are told that it isn't okay to express emotion; that emotional expression or vulnerability is weakness. Boys who do not conform to the "tough guy" image of manliness, or who express too much emotion are told that they are gay, too girly, or need to grow up. These social realities often leave men leading lives where they bottle up their emotions, thus becoming emotionally unavailable to their wives and children. The emotional barriers many men experience in their family relationships early in life often shape how they relate to and respond to God later in life.

Consequently, many men are afraid of expressing spiritual emotion publicly, praying in front of their wives and children, or sharing the Gospel with a friend. The problem is that too many men struggle with leading their households spiritually or effectively expressing their faith to their wives and children. Our family needs to sense that we have a genuine relationship with God and that we are not ashamed to share it or express it. Our family needs to sense that our relationship with God is secure in order to safely follow our spiritual leadership.

At the heart or core of spirituality is the extent to which one is determined to honor God in how they live. It is an acknowledgement or awareness that God is omnipotent (all powerful), omniscient (all knowing), and omnipresent (has no physical boundaries or limitations that can contain Him). As such, God deserves our worship and praise simply because of who He is. There are a variety of ways in which we can honor God.

It's important to know that as men we aren't all locked into a single form of spiritual expression that we should all follow. The most important questions we should ask ourselves are: Do I have a relationship with God? Am I determined to honor God in how I live my life? Am I afraid to communicate or express my faith and what I stand for as a man of God to my family and those around me?

Worship isn't about any particular style of spiritual expression, but instead, it is about living an obedient lifestyle before God. Worship isn't gender specific; it's biblical. I don't have to be afraid of expressing my spiritual relationship in any God-glorifying way that I see fit (e.g., crying, shouting, clapping my hands, singing, praying, lifting my hands, saying 'amen,' pumping my fist).

We often view worship as something that only spiritually "deep" people do. We often say it doesn't take all that. Listen, my brother, there isn't anything "deeper" than giving God the honor, glory, and praise by thanking Him for every little thing He has done in your life. Faith was never meant to be practiced in silence. God is not glorified when we neglect opportunities to honor Him when our family is watching us. Biblically mature men understand that their family needs to have tangible evidence of their relationship with God. Biblically mature men understand that God is their source; that God is the One who gave them life and that having a relationship is not an option but a requirement, if they are to make it in this world. The Apostle Paul expressed it this way: "…For in Him we live and move and exist" (Acts 17:28). Our family needs to witness our outward conviction and reliance on God. When they witness our relationship and devotion to God, they can sense spiritual security, and follow our lead.

Mature husbands and fathers give their wives and children the gift of spiritual security. They first demonstrate that they have a genuine relationship with God and that they have a personal conviction that God is the ultimate source of provision and the reason that all of the family's needs are met. Life was never supposed to be lived apart from God. I believe that we cannot properly fulfill our responsibilities as husbands and fathers unless we are in proper alignment with the Creator. We aren't designed, nor are we equipped to be good fathers or husbands outside of our spiritual connection with our Creator. Men who attempt to fulfill these roles outside of God, and in their own power and understanding, often find themselves experiencing frustration and stress.

Before the Fall, Adam was in perfect spiritual alignment with God. Life was easy—a literal cake walk. After the Fall, Adam was out of spiritual alignment with his Creator. Disconnected from God, life became hard, frustrating, and stressful for the first time in Adam's and Eve's lives (Genesis 3:16-19). Biblically mature men understand that they were never designed to do life apart from God. Instead, they understand that God is their ultimate source of provision and the One who graces them with the ability to provide for their family.

MATURE MEN ARE SELF-AWARE

Biblically mature men are self-aware. In other words, we have come to terms with the fact that we have personal limitations. Unlike Jesus, you and I will experience moments in our journey as fathers or husbands where we will fall short. There will be times when we fail to give our wife and children what they need. Being self-aware also means that we have a healthy view of ourselves. Self-aware men understand their limitations, but they also understand their strength and worth. They first and foremost view themselves as an integral part of their family, are cognizant of their role and function as heads of their households, and desire and strive to grow and develop into the fathers and husbands that God has called them to be.

Biblically mature fathers and husbands don't need to have all the answers. Nor do they need to have it all together. They only need to be willing to submit and to commit their lives in the hands of a loving God. It is God, and God alone who has promised to supply all of our need (Philippians 4:19). Perfect men don't exist; only men who recognize that they have inadequacies in the natural, but that they can put their full trust in a perfect God.

Knowing God personally and intimately, mature biblical men are aware that their family's greatest need is to be and feel spiritually secure. It is their family's desire to sense a connection to something bigger and greater than them. It is in these moments that there is nothing humanly possible that we can do to supply our family's need. When our full trust is in God, we can confidently point our wives and children in the direction of a holy, loving, and righteous God.

MATURE MEN ARE GOD AWARE

Biblically mature men have a healthy self-concept and provide spiritual security to their families when they demonstrate that they have a genuine relationship with God. Our families also feel spiritually secure when we make God a personal priority and are spiritually aware of His hand in our lives and in the lives of our wives and children. What I mean by God awareness is that we demonstrate to our family that we have an awareness or conviction that God is the ultimate source of provision and the reason that all of our family's needs are met.

Biblically mature men understand and clearly communicate to their families that everything that they have, and everything that they are as a family, ultimately comes from the Lord. They let their wife and children know that God is the One who graces us, empowers us, and enables us as husbands and fathers to provide for our households. They make a point to let their family know that it is by His grace and goodness that they have a roof over their heads, clothes on their backs, and food in their stomachs. They make a point to communicate to their family that God deserves all of the glory, all of the honor, and all of the praise.

I've got to communicate to my family that God is our source. My job isn't our source, my check isn't our source, nor is a person our source; but God alone is our source. It is by His hand and His grace that we have all that we need. Situations and circumstances may change, and there will be moments where we experience the highs and lows of life, but as a family, our trust will be placed in a faithful God who does not change. As husbands and fathers we must point to the Lord as our ultimate source and be sure to deny the temptation to compete for God's glory. When we present ourselves to our family as their ultimate source and convince ourselves and them that we are all that they need, we will always fail because there will be areas of need that our family has that we cannot meet on our own.

MODELING THE GIFT OF SPIRITUAL SECURITY

Our wives and children feel spiritually secure when they know that we know God on a personal level, and they see the fruits of our relationship with Him on a regular basis. Our wives and children need to witness us setting aside regular times of devotion, prayer, and moments to worship.

I try to live out my personal relationship with the Lord by showing my family a consistent example of a person who is trying to please God. I may not always get it right, but they come to realize that I am laser-focused on making God a priority in my personal life and I am not afraid to communicate this to my family through my words and actions. My family knows that I'm not schizophrenic with my faith. There aren't two Michaels: one at church on the pulpit on Sundays, and another at home. Over the years, they have witnessed my relationship with the Lord.

Your family needs to see your willingness to pray in public, to pray during meals, and to pray with them before they go to school. They need to see you lead in seeing to it that the family goes to church together and make a point to pray over and into the lives of your wife and children. They need to see you being sensitive to God and the things of God. Your children need to see you submitted to God and committed to honoring God in the way you live. Your family needs to see your vulnerability and view your life as a representation or model of a mature biblical man.

Furthermore, biblically mature men set the spiritual atmosphere of their house by inviting the presence of God and saturating their home environment in prayer. As stated in the prior chapter, ensuring that one's home is a safe and secure place for family relationships to flourish gives your wife and children emotional security. Likewise, to invite God's presence in your house and to cover one's family and home in prayer provides spiritual security. Brother, your prayer does not need to be complex or sound like someone who has been in church his entire life. God is less concerned with how long you pray, how loud you pray, or how many scriptures you quote while you pray. He is concerned about whether your heart is in the right place, and your prayer is genuine. Your prayer can be simple, yet honest and real. "Lord, I need you." "Lord, I need your help right now." "Lord, I don't understand this situation, I need clarity." "Lord, I feel hopeless and discouraged…this situation is out of my control." Whatever the prayer, it's important that our family see God as our supernatural source, our strength, and aide. When our family senses our spiritual security, they will trust us and follow our pattern of initiation placing their full trust in God.

Establishing a spiritual atmosphere of prayer and worship in your home means to set aside a private and intimate space or place that entices God's Spirit and guards from spiritual invasion. Such an environment should be a place where the biblical principles of God are practiced; where a family can safely raise their children in an atmosphere of faith. Mature men relate to God, hear from God, and speak to God. It is in this context that the space isn't just simply guarded in a physical sense, but it is also guarded in a spiritual sense. Mature husbands will both cover their homes and families in prayer and initiate a pattern of prayer and worship in their home and enrich the lives of their wives and children with the Word of God. The greatest gift a father can give his family is the gift of spiritual security or a deep and personal relationship with God. Mature husbands and fathers set the spiritual tone of their homes by making their relationship with God a priority in their personal lives, marriage, and family relationships. When mature biblical men initiate times of prayer, devotion, and worship, and model a consistent spiritual example to their wives and children, their families will inevitably follow suit and view the Lord as their ultimate source.

When my wife, Twanna, was pregnant with our son, MJ, she constantly listened to the Bible and various messages on CD. I believe that it was during that time that our special needs son began to develop a bond and appreciation for the Word of God. MJ has witnessed his parents praying, studying, and listening to the Bible, watching various religious broadcasts, and trusting God through the challenging moments of our lives. My wife and I bought MJ an iPad. His favorite app to use is the audio Bible app. Sometimes when MJ feels nervous or uncomfortable, he will grab his iPad, head to his room and listen to the Bible. MJ can listen to the Bible for hours on end and never get tired of it. What's amazing is the calming effect that the Bible has on MJ. Although MJ is only eleven and is special needs, he both understands and embraces that we are a family that loves and trusts in the Lord. MJ's response is the direct result of the spiritual environment that my wife and I set in our home, and the extent to which we make our spiritual lives an open book to one another.

DISTORTED MASCULINITY:
SOCIETY VS. GOD'S WORD

Society says I need no one; God's Word says I need God (Acts 17:28). Society says manhood is tied to what I have; God's Word says that manhood is tied to who I am in Him (Psalm 1:1-3). Society says it is the man's responsibility to put food on the table; God's Word says that I need not neglect to give my family the bread of life or the Word of God (Ephesians 5:26; Ephesians 6:4; Deuteronomy 6:7; Proverbs 22:6). Society says I am my wife and children's source; God's Word says God is my family's source and I have to draw from His strength to properly function as a husband and father (Psalm 1:1-3; Ephesians 6:10; Psalm 118:14).

The enemy, whether you realize it or not, has a hit out on men. In the Garden, he wasn't coming for Adam, per se; he was coming for the spiritual alignment and connection Adam had with his God. Let me tell you a secret that the enemy doesn't want you to know: When man spiritually aligns himself with his God there is no devil in hell or man or woman on earth who can stop him. We see this in the life of Jesus Christ: although Satan tried, he was unable to break the spiritual connection between the Son and his Father. In failing to do so, Jesus successfully accomplished what He was placed on this earth to do. If we begin to get in spiritual alignment with God and all that He has for us, I believe that we too, will find that there is nothing that the devil can do to stop us and our family from accomplishing what we've been placed on this earth to do.

THE CHALLENGE

I would like to challenge you to consider the impact that your father did or did not have in your life. Consider where you are and who you are, today, as a person. How did your relationship with your father alter your life for better or worse? Much of our life experiences, personal troubles, and triumphs were linked to whether our father was engaged in our lives or not. Some of us are still dealing with the consequences or benefits of their engagement and the extent to which we felt financially, materially, emotionally, and spiritually secure. The security that our wives and children sense is a by-product of the extent to which we supply for them (provide) what they need.

As our father's presence or absence mattered in the trajectory of our lives, our presence and financial-emotional-spiritual engagement matters in the lives our children and wives. Our family needs more than our money and material resources. They need our intimate involvement and engagement in their lives. Our family needs to see deep inside our heart. They need to see more than our physical presence; we need to have an emotional presence. Our wives and children need intimacy (in-to-me-you-see). They need to see our vulnerability. They need to see us being naked, open, and transparent in their presence; sharing our fears, apprehensions, failures, wisdom, and experiences. They need to feel connected to us. Finally, they need to sense that we have a genuine relationship with the Lord and that we view God as our ultimate source of provision.

The reality is that no man is perfect and will not fulfill all of these needs completely. It's important, however, to understand where the biblical mark is, and strive to grow and develop in meeting the needs of our families. This isn't to say that what I've outlined here is an exhaustive list of what families need. Families may need more than financial, emotional, and spiritual security, but certainly not less. God the Father truly took it upon Himself to be whatever man needed. We need to be flexible enough as husbands and fathers to do the same for our families, recognizing and discerning their greatest area of need from moment to moment. Sometimes what our wives may need the most, for instance, is for us to see to it that money is set aside for them to get their hair and nails done or pay for them to get a surprise massage because we sense that they are a bit stressed (financial and material security). Other times, our children may need to hear us say: "I love you," "I'm proud of you," or simply "How are things going?" (emotional security). In other moments, our wives and children may simply need to hear us praying and asking God to bless and protect our family early in the morning or, perhaps, declaring that God is our source and that we as a family will stand firm on the Word of God during difficult times (spiritual security).

This is threefold biblical provision. Mature men make it their priority to provide their wife and children with financial security, emotional security, and spiritual security. In so doing, we give our wives and children what they need.

PART IV

Husbands and Fathers as Protectors of Their Households

When I was a boy, Superman, known as the Man of Steel, mesmerized me. Superman was an iconic figure whose physical strength was unmatched and whose speed and power was without limits. I remember the television series announcer blaring Superman's description as being "faster than a speeding bullet, more powerful than a locomotive... able to leap tall buildings in a single bound!" Fighting a "never-ending battle for truth, justice, and freedom with superpowers," Superman was a class act, an American super hero, and a man's man!

Like most superheroes however, Superman wasn't completely invincible. He had one weakness:

Kryptonite. A fictional radioactive element from the planet Krypton, Kryptonite caused Superman to lose his superhuman strength, speed, and agility. As I reflect on my childhood icon, I am reminded of the limits of my own physical/brute strength. Even in the context of a superhuman body, Superman's physical strength was no match for a small, green, unassuming crystal shard.

Like Superman, good husbands and fathers need to understand the limitations of their own physical strength. To properly protect their families biblically, it requires protecting and guarding their families in a spiritual sense. Biblically mature men understand that God has charged them to be the first line of spiritual defense in their homes by covering their wives, children, and households in prayer which enables them to ward off spiritual/demonic attacks with the Word of God. In so doing, mature husbands and fathers properly protect their families and households from physical AND spiritual harm.

In this final section of the book, I want to discuss the third biblical responsibility of Godly men which is as Protectors. I want to begin by highlighting God's expectation for Adam as the designated physical-spiritual protector of his family, and then end with a discussion of what twenty-first century men can learn from Adam's failure as a physical-spiritual Protector as we strive to become mature biblical Protectors of our homes.

Godly fathers and husbands strive to protect across at least two dimensions. These two dimensions are: first, by protecting their wives and children from physical harm, even if it means standing in harm's way with our very lives (Chapter 12); and second, by protecting their wives and children from spiritual harm or spiritual attack by covering our families/homes in prayer and using the Word of God as our weapon against demonic attack (Chapter 13). Mature husbands and fathers both understand and embrace the biblical mandate on their lives to defend their families from both physical and spiritual invasion/ attack to the best of their abilities.

CHAPTER 12 ───────

Protecting Your Family From Physical Harm and Danger

God commanded Adam to "cultivate" and "keep" the garden (Genesis 2:15). As stated in earlier chapters, the Hebrew word for "cultivate" is *abad,* which means to work, labor, and till the ground. The Hebrew word for "keep" however is *shamar,* which can best be interpreted to mean to guard, have charge of, protect, and watch over. In other words, Adam's responsibility in this context was two fold: (1) to provide for his family by laboring with his hands as highlighted in the prior section of this book; and (2) to guard or protect his home from harm, danger, and intrusion, as will be discussed over the next two chapters. In a biblical sense, God viewed Adam's responsibility as a cultivator (provider) and keeper (protector) of the garden as an assignment or work done unto the Lord. This wasn't simply a *job* in the sense that God was giving Adam something to do, but rather a vocation in the sense that God was giving Adam an *assignment* or divine life calling that he was expected to fulfill as a husband and future father.

ADAM'S LIFE CALLING: PROTECTOR OF THE HOME

Adam's life calling as a Protector was physical in the sense that Adam was positioned to represent the first line of defense against physical attack on his family and physical intrusion in his home. It was also spiritual in the sense that Adam had an intimate relationship with God, and it was through this relationship that God gave explicit instructions or boundaries by which Adam and his family were supposed to live (His Word). In Genesis 2:16-17, God commanded Adam saying, "From any tree of the garden you may eat freely, but from the tree of the knowledge of good or evil you shall not eat, for in the day that you eat from it you will surely die (NASB)." Notice that God's directive was only to Adam (Eve was yet to be created) and God's command was clear in the sense that He expected Adam to obey His Word and fully understand the eternal consequences of disregarding His command (death). Given that Eve was missing in action and there is no biblical evidence to suggest that Eve had first hand knowledge of God's instructions regarding the tree of the knowledge of good and evil, we can safely assume that the Creator gave Adam the responsibility to communicate and declare the boundaries He laid out (His Word) to his wife and future children.

ADAM'S FAILURE AS A PROTECTOR

Adam fell short as a Protector in at least three ways. First, Adam carelessly allowed the devil to set up camp in his domain (the garden). God made Adam the guardian of Eden and gave him authority to protect his dwelling place from physical and spiritual attack (Genesis 1:26, 28b; 2:15-16). Second, Adam carelessly allowed the devil to establish rapport with his wife (Genesis 3:1-7). The third chapter of Genesis implies that Adam was fully aware of the dialogue between his wife and serpent, yet he stood by passively. Genesis 3:6 states, "When the woman saw that the tree was good for food, and that it was a delight to the eye, and that the tree was desirable to make one wise, she took from its fruit and ate and she gave also to her husband *with her* and he ate. The Hebrew word for with (*im*) here doesn't mean with in a general or distant sense, it means *beside* or *alongside*. In other words, Adam was with or beside Eve while she was being deceived. Instead of defending God's word and reminding his wife of God's pre-established boundaries in the garden (Genesis 2:16-17), Adam chose to passively acquiesce to Eve's invitation to sin and disobey God. Adam had the capacity to tell Eve, "No, honey that is not in line with God's Word," or tell her that "God said the consequences of rebelling against His Word is death." Adam did none of this.

It is unclear whether Adam's response to his wife's indiscretion was the result of: (1) fear in the sense that he was afraid of Eve's potentially negative response to his refusal; (2) his desire to seek his wife's acceptance in that he was more concerned with pleasing his wife than honoring God; or (3) confusion/deception in that he was genuinely misled by the serpent to disobey God.

Regardless of the circumstances, it is clear that Adam heard and received a personal warning from God that the fruit from the tree of the knowledge of good and evil was off limits. Instead of digging his heels in the ground and defending the Word of God and saying "as for me and my house we will serve the Lord" (Joshua 24:15), Adam idly stood by and allowed the very person he was put on this earth to protect be taken advantage of and manipulated by Satan.

As a result of Adam's passivity and failure in leadership, he and his wife were kicked out of the garden (Genesis 3:23-24) and experienced spiritual separation from God's presence and protection or divine covering. God's covering operated as a spiritual shield or umbrella that gave Adam and Eve a sense of spiritual security (Psalm 91:4). After the Fall, God's spiritual covering was removed and Adam and Eve felt uncovered or naked and sensed an immediate need to cover themselves (Genesis 3:7). In the garden, most theologians agree that Adam and Eve would have lived forever (Genesis 3:22). Outside of the garden, Adam and Eve would surely die.

BIBLICAL FATHERS AND HUSBANDS AS PROTECTORS

God charged Adam with the responsibility to keep or protect all life that dwelled in the garden. Likewise, God endows husbands and fathers with the same capacity today. For some of you reading this, you may say that this is ludicrous. The independent women of today are well able to care for and protect themselves. They don't need a man to protect them even in the context of marriage, right? My response: this was exactly God's intent from the beginning. Although it's the case that male-female relations, generally speaking, and marital relationships in particular have been distorted since the Fall, this distortion doesn't change the relevancy of the Word of God today. The principle here is that God gives husbands the responsibility to protect their wives. This responsibility does not devalue their personhood. Instead, it is a biblical reality that although men and women were called to co-rule and are of equal spiritual value, they differ in unique ways physically and emotionally. The Apostle Peter communicates this point in 1 Peter 3:7 as he highlights that although women are "weaker," or more physically and emotionally vulnerable than men, they are "equal partners in God's gift of (eternal) life" (NLT).

This isn't to say that women are altogether *weak*. Few husbands who have watched their wives give birth would voluntarily take their place on a hospital bed and endure multiple hours of labor, poking, and prodding. Rather, it was the Apostle Peter's intent to point out that men and women are different. Along emotional and physical lines for instance, women are typically more fragile and husbands need to be sensitive to and mindful of their vulnerability and need for protection or covering.

I spent a great deal of time in the prior section of the book discussing the importance of giving our wives and children emotional security and I won't repeat that here. It is important to remember that as we protect our wives emotionally, we have to be careful to guard their hearts and deal with them in an understanding and loving way given their emotional vulnerability (1 Peter 3:7; Colossians 3:19; Ephesians 5:28-30).

In terms of protecting women physically, the physical vulnerability of women at a societal level is clearly underscored when we consider national arrest data collected by the FBI. This data overwhelmingly demonstrates a pattern of male aggression and female victimization. Consider, for instance, that while men encompass less than 50%[1] of the U.S. population, we commit and are arrested for 89% of all murders, 87% of all robberies and more than 99% of all officially reported rapes.[2]

Compared to their male counterparts however, women are four times more likely to be the victims of intimate partner violence.[3] Such sobering statistics make clear a female's physical vulnerability and the great need for men to protect the women in their lives.

PHYSICAL NEED: REAL MEN ALWAYS COME TO THE RESCUE

Whether we realize it or not, men grow up with a

super hero complex. We often come into marriage with the expectation that we are going to fix stuff. We are problem-solvers. Our wives come to us with a need, and we have a solution…dah dah dah…off to the rescue! Like Superman, we get the importance of (physically) protecting our home. It comes natural to many of us. You, like myself, have probably been told your entire life that real men protect women — that's the honorable and chivalrous thing to do. When men don't have a natural motivation to protect women and/or would be willing to put women in harm's way to protect themselves, it is a strong sign that their sense of manhood or masculinity is distorted and immature. As Pastor John Piper states regarding biblically mature men:

> Mature masculinity senses a natural, God-given responsibility to step forward and put [oneself] between an assailant and [a] woman…his inner sense is one of responsibility to protect her because he is a man and she is a woman. There is a distorted and sinful masculinity that might claim authority and leadership that has the right to tell the woman to step in front of him to shield him from the blows and let him escape. But every man knows this is a perversion of what it means to be a man and a leader. And every wife knows that something is amiss in a man's manhood if he suggests that she get

out of the bed 50% of the time to see what the strange noise is downstairs (p. 43).[4]

Mature men are willing to suffer and/or place themselves in harm's way for women because they have an understanding that females are to be honored and cherished. We are to use our God-given strength to protect our wives (and children). Our family should know that we are willing to protect them even if it means protecting them with our very lives.

In a practical sense, mature biblical men should take it upon themselves to make sure that doors in their homes are locked and their cars are secured. They should feel a level of uneasiness when their wives or children are out late at night and make a point to ensure that they've made it safely to their destination and that they make it safely back home. Mature husbands and fathers should run to the aid of their wives and children when people attempt to abuse them or take advantage of them whether the potential abuser is a mechanic, clerk, business person, or someone meaning to do them physical harm such as a sexual predator, co-worker, or another family member.

As husbands and fathers, God has endowed us with the capacity to protect our children and family from physical harm, danger, and intrusion. When we are actively involved in disciplining and giving our children boundaries, and protecting our home from intruders, our presence acts as a shield that gives our wives and children a sense of physical security. What I mean is that people will be less likely to approach our family, or attempt to use, abuse, or take advantage of them. We send a message that our family is protected and that 'if you want to get to my family you have to go through me first — I am the first line of defense.'

Although I am calling for men to be vigilante Protectors of their home, what I am not suggesting is that we should become controlling or manipulative in our leadership or protection. Manipulation and controlling actions do not reflect loving leadership. Rather we need to work with our wives or children's mother to set clear guidelines for our children and let them know that these guidelines are for their good. In the case of our wives, we need to avoid making our wives feel like a child through our protection and be sure that they sense that the motive behind our protection is love. Finally, as Protectors of our home, we need to make clear to our family that the Word of God provides the boundaries by which the family must live and we need to make a priority covering our family in prayer. In other words, we should spend less time worrying and more time praying. As Philippians 4:6 reminds us: "Don't worry about anything; instead, pray about everything. Tell God what you need, and thank him for all he has done"

(NLT).

This leads us into the second dimension of biblical protection. Godly fathers and husbands provide spiritual protection to their family through covering their family and household in prayer and declaring the Word of God to those under their care.

Footnotes

[1]   U.S. Census Bureau. 2014. Annual Estimates of the Resident Population for Selected Age Groups by Sex for the United States, States, Counties, and Puerto Rico Commonwealth and Municipios: April 1, 2010 to July 1, 2013.

[2]   Federal Bureau of Investigation [FBI], 2012. Crime in the United States, 2012 (Table 35). Retrieved from: http://www.fbi.gov/about-us/cjis/ucr/crime-in-the-u.s/2012/crime-in-the-u.s.-2012/tables/35tabledatadecoverviewpdf

3   Bureau of Justice Statistics [BJS]. September 2011. Criminal Victimization, 2010 (Figure 6). Retrieved from: http://www.bjs.gov/content/pub/pdf/cv10.pdf

[4]   Piper, John. "A Vision of Biblical Complementarity." *Recovering Biblical Manhood and Womanhood: A Response to Evangelical Feminism.* Ed. John Piper and Wayne Grudem. Wheaton, Illinois: Crossway, 2006 (Second Edition). 31-59.

CHAPTER 13 ———

Providing a Spiritual Covering for Your Family

Like most men, I have had my share of gym memberships, weight rooms, treadmills, and sweat suits in order to build my physical strength *and look good for my woman!* However, I have discovered that there is no amount of time in the gym that can possibly prepare you as a husband and/or father to defend your home or protect your wife and children from spiritual or demonic attack. Biblically mature men understand the limitations of their physical strength. There is a spiritual world and a spiritual battle between good and evil that is beyond our physical capacity and control. As the Apostle Paul reminds us in Ephesians 6:10-12: "...*Be strong in the Lord and in His mighty power.*

Put on all of God's armor so that you will be able to stand firm against all strategies of the devil. For we are not fighting against flesh-and-blood enemies, but against evil rulers and authorities of the unseen world, against mighty powers in this dark world, and against evil spirits in the heavenly places" (NLT).

If I want to properly protect my household from the various spiritual forces and influences at play, my biceps, triceps, boxing skills, or street knowledge won't help me. I have to be strong in God's power and not my own. I have to put on God's armor and not make the mistake of attempting to fight a spiritual war with an earthly arsenal. I have to live a disciplined lifestyle and develop spiritual weapons such as praying, fasting, studying and speaking/declaring God's Word and applying it to my life. Living a biblically disciplined lifestyle looks like "exercising daily" in your relationship with God and becoming fit in the Word of God (1 Timothy 4:8, The Message).

In a practical sense, biblically mature men protect their families from spiritual/demonic attack by: (1) being watchmen and guards of their households against spiritual attack for their wives and children, and (2) covering their wives and children in prayer.

SPIRITUAL INFLUENCES AND OPEN DOORS

A spiritual influence is any potential negative influence or intruder that can draw us away from our relationship with God. These are influences that can enter our homes by way of a direct personal spiritual attack, or more indirectly, in the form of a spiritual attack on one of our family members, friends, or anyone who is connected to us. As the devil used Eve to cause Adam to disobey God, he will attempt to use your family and others to launch a spiritual attack on you.

Spiritual influences generally enter our homes by way of a symbolic open door. After the Fall of Adam and Eve, Genesis 4 fast-forwards to the story of their sons, Cain and Abel. Abel was a shepherd, and his older brother Cain was a farmer, having the occupation of one who "cultivated the ground" (Genesis 4:2, NLT). When it was harvest time, Cain presented *some* of his crops as a gift to the Lord. In contrast, Abel brought the *best portions* of the firstborn lambs from his flock. The Lord accepted Abel's gift but rejected Cain's. Cain became very angry by this, and the Lord's reply to his anger is very telling. He said:

> "Why are you so angry...why do you look so dejected? You will be accepted if you do what

is right. But if you refuse to do what is right, then watch out! *Sin is crouching at the door, eager to control you.* But you must subdue it and be its master" (Genesis 4:6-7, NIV).

The principle here is two-fold. First, it is often through our disobedience or moral rebellion to God (sin) that we *open the door* to demonic or spiritual influence. Second, demonic and spiritual influence doesn't simply desire to hinder or distract us from our relationship with God. Its ultimate desire is to wreak havoc in our lives through its control/domination and destruction. This is what Jesus meant when he said the enemy's "purpose is to kill and steal and destroy" (John 10:10, NLT).

ACCESS GRANTED: OUR SIN AND DEMONIC/SPIRITUAL INFLUENCES

As husbands and fathers, one of the most common ways to open ourselves and our families to spiritual/demonic attack is by allowing them in our home through our own sin. For Cain, his open door was anger. For us, our open door may be pornography, (emotional or sexual) affairs that we've initiated outside the home, alcoholism, or other secret struggles or sins that we've not dealt with or confessed. As men, it is crucial that we do not allow the enemy's tactics to lure us and trap us. The enemy needs only a crack in the door, then before you know it, he has kicked the door open to your sin issue! There is perhaps no surer way to remove God's spiritual covering (protection) and to block His blessings and favor from our lives than by attempting to conceal unconfessed sin. I know that it can be very difficult for us to trust another person with our vulnerabilities, but I have learned over the years, that having another godly brother in my life for accountability has helped me tremendously. Proverbs 28:13 is clear: "People who conceal their sins will not prosper, but if they confess and turn from them, they will receive mercy" (NLT). When we struggle or attempt to conceal unconfessed sin, our wives and children may often suffer. The popular blogger and author Tim Challies makes clear this point in his article titled, "Leadership in the Home: A Godly Man Protects." Challies states:

> One of the unmistakable lessons we learn from reading the Old Testament is that a nation can suffer because of the sin of its leader and that a family can suffer because of the sin of its father. When Achan sinned (Joshua 7) by keeping for himself some of the items plundered from Jericho that God had devoted for his own use, it was not only Achan who suffered the consequences. All of Israel was

punished for a time through the disastrous battle of Ai which saw thirty-six soldiers fall as the Israelite army was routed. God revealed that one man had sin and eventually Achan's whole family was put to death for the sin of the father. "They burned them with fire and stoned them with stones." Think as well of the rebellion of Korah as described in Numbers 16. Korah rebelled against Moses' leadership, saying that he was exalting himself beyond the rest of the people. God's judgment was swift: "And as soon as he had finished speaking all these words, the ground under them split apart. And the earth opened its mouth and swallowed them up, with their households and all the people who belonged to Korah and all their goods." In both cases, the husband and father sinned but the whole family suffered consequences.[1]

This may seem unfair to some women and children, but God takes seriously a husband's/father's responsibility to protect and provide a covering for their families. When husbands are out of their God-ordained positions as protectors and guardians of their homes, the entire family is vulnerable. As a side note, this does not mean that every home in which a husband-father has unrepented sin goes uncovered. 1 Corinthians 7:14 reminds us that *a godly wife sanctifies her husband and children.* In other words, God doesn't leave these homes completely uncovered as a result of the prayers and righteous living of a believing wife.

PROTECTING OUR WIVES AND CHILDREN

We protect or guard our wives and children by being watchful to the potential negative spiritual influences that may harm our relationship with God and/or our relationship with those in our household. As discussed in the section on husbands and fathers as godly providers, God ordained the family as an important institution that ensures many of our needs are met (e.g. material/financial, emotional, physical). Likewise, a relationship with God meets perhaps our greatest need (spiritual need) and also other areas of need that we may lack (Philippians 4:19). When our wives and children have what they need, they feel a sense of security and they are less likely to seek to have their needs met through other people and things outside of their home. In cases where our wives' or children's needs are not met, the probability of our family members going outside of the home to meet one's needs significantly increases.

As protectors and guardians of our homes, it is critical that we pay attention to our personal/spiritual needs and the nature of the relationships that we develop outside our home (e.g. co-workers, colleagues or others we interact with). When we (or our wives) feel that we are not getting what we need in our marriage (e.g. emotional needs, sexual/physical needs, respect), it's very possible to develop unhealthy relationships outside of the home. These unhealthy relationships often provide an open door to emotional or sexual affairs and spiritual/demonic influence. As husbands, when we find ourselves developing an emotional attachment or if another woman is developing an emotional attachment to us, the first thing we should do is pull away. Run, Forrest, Run! There is no such a thing as *harmless* flirting with a woman whom you are not married to. Jesus made no distinction between emotional and sexual affairs (Matthew 5:28). In both cases, these behaviors represent sinful acts and open doors to spiritual/demonic influence that has the potential to break-up your marriage and destroy your family. Satan is looking for an opportunity to take you out — don't give him one! Don't be naïve to think that the enemy won't use any available person, whether it is a co-worker, friend, member of your church, past relation, or ex-girlfriend to launch a spiritual attack or assault on your home. The enemy is looking for an open door, roaming around the earth like a lion seeking whom he may attack (1 Peter 5:8).

Here are a few questions you need to ask yourself: Are you opening doors thereby leaving your family vulnerable due to your disobedience? Or are you closing doors with your obedience? Are you inviting God's presence and spiritual covering over your household by living a life of biblical integrity? Or are you rejecting God's presence and covering by your deception and unconfessed sin?

In addition to being on guard about potential affairs, we need to also be on guard regarding male friendships. If we are always running out of the house to hangout with male friends, we should ask ourselves: What am I running from? Are my children constantly asking 'where is daddy'? Is my wife wondering where I am when I should be home? You cannot protect (or love) your wife in the way that she desires if you are never home.

You cannot properly protect your child or children if they are left fatherless (raising themselves). If we are barely around, are always running out of the house, or we are present, but disconnected and uninvolved, our wives and children may feel insecure in our love, care and protection. I am not saying that it is a bad thing to have healthy male friendships and go out with the boys every once in a while. It is a good thing to connect with other men. What I am saying, however, is that we need to fight to be a presence in the lives of our wives and children. Our family needs us, and if we are never around they will never get all that they need or deserve from us. For our wives, if we are always missing in action, it becomes a breeding ground for divorce or separation. For children, it may lead to waywardness as children will feel that they don't have the love, support, and time that they so desperately need from both parents. In both cases, we are essentially leaving our wives and children uncovered and vulnerable to spiritual/demonic attack.

PROTECTING OUR CHILDREN IN THE 21ST CENTURY – WHAT YOU SHOULD KNOW

Godly fathers do whatever is necessary to protect their wives and children from invasion outside of the home. As Tim Challies highlights:

> You must [as a father] be constantly aware, constantly on guard against danger your family may encounter...you will need to take the lead in ensuring that your children are using the internet wisely, that you have criteria for protecting your children from predators online or offline, that they are not encountering things on television that their minds and hearts are not yet equipped to understand.[2]

In the 21st century, one of the biggest threats to the minds of our children is technology. Our inability to safeguard and monitor what our children are watching on television, the websites that they are visiting throughout the week, and the information they are exposed to and are sharing on entertainment/social media sites (e.g. YouTube, Vine, Facebook, Twitter, Instagram, etc.) is having a grave impact on our homes and our relationships with our children. It is extremely important as fathers that we embrace and learn how to use today's technology so that we can also safeguard our children's access to inappropriate media/internet content. A 2010 study done by the Kaiser Family Foundation found that children between the ages of 8 to 18 spend roughly 7 hours and 38 minutes using entertainment media across a typical day.[3] Because most young people multitask (using more than one media medium at a time), they actually pack about 11 hours of media entertainment into a single day. The same study also found that 70% of these children reported that they have **no rules** on how much time they can spend watching TV, playing video games, and using computers. When the study examined the grades of these kids, they found that nearly 47% of high media consumers reported having grades that were fair or poor compared to 23% of light users. African-American and Hispanic children consumed on average 4.5 additional hours of media compared to White children.

These findings highlight the necessity of us as fathers taking the lead in restricting and monitoring our children's access to technology. It also raises the question: if American children on average are consuming media for longer amounts of time than we spend at work, and they are also spending most of their waking hours on their cell phones, iPads, computers, etc., who has the greatest influence on our children's values and worldview: us or the media they are exposed to? If we neglect keeping ourselves informed about the technology available to our children, we leave our children uncovered and vulnerable to spiritual-mental invasion on our watch.

SPIRITUAL WARFARE

The most important lesson of this chapter is one that Christian author and missionary C. Peter Wagner made several decades ago in his book titled, *Warfare Prayer: How to Seek God's Power and Protection in the Battle to Build His Kingdom*. Wagner wrote, "Satan's power never has been nor ever will be a match for the power of God."[4] We don't defeat the enemy and demonic forces based on our own ability…but rather through the power and authority of the Holy Spirit.

The Apostle Paul continued in his encouragement to the church of Ephesus by communicating the importance of putting on the full armor of God in order to defeat the enemy's schemes. The full armor of God consists of the following items: the belt of truth, breastplate of righteousness, shoes with the preparation of the gospel of peace, shield of faith, helmet of salvation, and the sword of the spirit which is the Word of God (Ephesians 6:14-17). Paul concludes this thought regarding spiritual warfare in verses 17 and 18 of the sixth chapter of Ephesians when he states: "...[use] the sword of the Spirit, which is the word of God. Pray in the Spirit at all times and on every occasion..." (Ephesians 6:17b-18, NLT). As the The Message Bible version of these verses highlights: "God's Word is an *indispensable* weapon. In the same way, prayer is essential in this ongoing warfare" (Ephesians 6:17-18, Message). Based on these verses, it is easy to conclude that the two spiritual weapons that we have at our disposal are the Word of God (also referred to as the sword of the spirit) and Prayer. All other military apparel associated with the full armor of God are related to spiritual defense. I would argue, however, that this is not the Apostle Paul's intent here. Paul is pointing out that in spiritual warfare we only have one weapon: the Holy Spirit. The Holy Spirit is the power source or engine by which we tear down strongholds. Prayer without the help of the Holy Spirit is just talking. Reading the Word of God without the Holy Spirit to illuminate your understanding is like reading a foreign language. You won't understand it, and you cannot properly apply it to your life.

In a practical sense, biblically mature men cover their wives and children in prayer. This looks like committing to a regular time to commune with and pray to God. This also looks like praying over your wife and children at night and praying over them in the morning. It looks like praying over your children before you drop them off at school and praying with your wife when she awakes. It looks like daily going into the spiritual realm and disrupting the enemy's tactics, strategies,and schemes. It looks like praying for your family's future and destiny.

Mature men also protect their family by teaching their children and encouraging their wife to follow their pattern of initiation as a prayer warrior of their home. When their wives or children find themselves in trouble or are in need of prayer, they understand the urgency of going to God themselves. When we do this, we prepare our children for the world so that they can become emotionally and spiritually healthy young adults who make good decisions with a worldview that lines up with the Word of God.

Finally, when hard times come or family tragedy strikes, mature men are slow to worry or stress and are quick to go to God for understanding, discernment, direction, and comfort. Adam was afraid to stand up, defend, and declare God's Word to his wife when the opportunity availed itself. He chose to be passive. In other words, he allowed the devil to bind him (Matthew 12:29). In binding him, he allowed the enemy to wreak havoc on his home and he lost all that God had given him. Afterwards, he found himself running away from God's presence for help instead of running to it. Protectors protect all that God gives them, and they fight for God's presence. Mature men do not shy away from opportunities to pray for and with their wives and children. In fact, they are quick to pray and are the first to initiate prayer because they understand that the prayer of the righteous works (James 5:16)!

Footnotes

[1] Challies, Tim. December 2009. "Leadership in the Home a Godly Man Protects." Blog. Retrieved from: http://www.challies.com/christian-living/leadership-in-the-home-a-godly-man-protects

[2] See footnote 1

3 The Henry J. Kaiser Family Foundation. 2010. Generation M^2: Media in the Lives of 8 to 18-year Olds. Menlo Park, California.

4 Wagner, C. Peter. *Warfare Prayer : How to Seek God's Power and Protection in the Battle to Build His Kingdom.* Gospel Light Publications. 1992.

CONCLUSION

Becoming a Good Man

Today, God's call to the Adams of this generation is a divine call for men to waken from the lull of materialism and complacency, and operate in our biblical responsibility as men to be leaders, providers, and protectors of our households. Adam failed because he ran from God's presence. Adam didn't come looking for the Creator to fix the crisis in the Garden. He tried to do it himself, attempting to cover the consequences of his sin with fig leaves (Genesis 3:7) and excuses (Genesis 3:12). In other words, instead of taking full responsibility, Adam chose to complicate his mistakes by making more mistakes to cover his sin. I believe God is calling the Adams of this generation to run to His presence and answer the call to take our rightful place in our families, communities, and churches.

GOOD MEN AREN'T BORN THEY ARE MADE

Adam made a lot of mistakes, and truthfully, we all have! The process of becoming a good man may seem unattainable, but that is the furthest thing from the truth. Good men aren't born; they are made. They are nurtured through mentorship and developed in the context of community. It's critical that we seek out mature Godly men to mentor and develop us into the husbands and fathers that we are called to be. Our journey of becoming a good man cannot be done alone. We need to find a community of biblically mature men, a men's ministry or men's group to provide support, hold us accountable and help us grow as we pursue becoming the men that God has created us to be. Accountability looks like being transparent and willing to open my heart and life to another mature man who I trust and look up to. This mentor should have my permission to challenge me and shine the light of the Word of God in the dark and spiritually stagnant places of my life.

Let's be real, we have too many "Yes" men and male cheerleaders in our lives. Men who support us and cheerlead us in our mess and struggles...men who are quick to tell us what we want to hear, but are slow to give us what we really need. We need strong men and mentors in our lives that are willing to speak the truth to us in love (even when it hurts). We need men in our corner who are willing to make an investment in our spiritual-emotional growth and are committed to motivating us to reach our full God-given potential.

MATURE MEN, STAND UP!

Listen up mature men…God has called you to use your gifts and talents to make a difference! Regardless of your marital status, age or whether you are a father or not, I challenge you to take your rightful place as a mature man in your families as strong fathers, grandfathers, uncles, brothers or cousins and committed mentors to young boys and girls in your community who lack a Godly male influence in their lives. Consider connecting with or beginning your own mentoring program, working with boys at-risk, connecting with young boys in your neighborhood, volunteering your knowledge or expertise to young children in the school system, at your local church, Boys and Girls Club or YMCA. Your presence is needed! I want to encourage you to get into position and walk in your purpose. I want to encourage you to give back and be a blessing to young boys in the prison system or as a coach to children for Little League, Pop Warner or some other competitive team sport. Your voice is needed! Your story, time and sacrifice may make a powerful difference in the destiny of a young boy. Your words of encouragement and direction may be exactly what a young boy needs to develop into a young man who is confident in who he is and what he has been placed on this earth to do! This is what true discipleship looks like. When people have made a difference in our lives, God calls us to reach back and make a difference in the life of someone else (Luke 22:32; Psalm 51:13).

IN WITH THE NEW (MAN), OUT WITH THE OLD (MAN)

Therefore, if any man be in Christ, he is a new creature: old things are passed away; behold, all things are become new (2 Corinthians 5:17). Above all, the greatest resource that a maturing man can have is a relationship with the Lord. When we invite the Lord into our life, we become a new creation in Him (2 Corinthians 5:17). The old man did not protect his family. The new (good) man would die for his family.

"When I was a child, I spake as a child, I understood as a child, I thought as a child: but when I became a man, I put away childish things" (1 Corinthians 13:11). I remember when my son, MJ, was born. My wife was admitted to the hospital early after developing preeclampsia (which is pregnancy induced hypertension). She was twenty-five weeks pregnant. (Forty weeks is a full term). The doctor came into her room and told us that he would have to perform an emergency c-section. He said that my son's chances of survival were minimal. Brother, I do not care who you are, when you get news like that, it is like a sucker punch has been thrown your way, and you are trying to steady yourself! My mind was racing, my heart was beating fast, and for a moment, I was gripped in fear. Then, almost immediately, I heard the Holy Spirit say in my spirit, *trust and believe.* I began to pray like I had never prayed before. In fact, I cried out to God because I knew that this was not a time to display my swag. My son's life was on the line! In fact, the doctor said that my wife could experience complications that could put her life in jeopardy as well. I began to intercede on behalf of my wife. I NEVER prayed so hard in my life before! I did not know if I would lose my wife (who is my best friend), and my only son. I prayed harder. My son was born that day at one pound, one ounce. It was a difficult and trying time for us.

"For we know in part, and we prophesy in part. But when that which is perfect is come, then that which is in part shall be done away" (1 Corinthians 13:9-10). I learned during that time that I did not need to be perfect. I did not even need to have all the answers. I needed to be present. I needed to encourage my wife. I needed to be strong in the Lord. And I needed to pray fervently to Him. You will encounter challenges in your life, but rest assured, God will come alongside you to give you what you need at that time when you call upon Him. We are imperfect, we are incomplete…BUT God makes the difference in our lives!

Brother, a GOOD MAN does not have to be hard to find. God has given us EVERYTHING that we need to be what He has called us to be (2 Peter 1:3). I do not have all the answers. But I do know what His word entitles us to. And God is not a respecter of persons (Acts 10:34). In other words, all of us have the capacity to be GOOD MEN. Our job is to seek God through His Word, learn from Adam's mistakes, and take our rightful positions. And as we grow in His word, then we are to teach His word to our sons and daughters. Adam hid because of his shame, his embarrassment, and his sin. We no longer have to walk in his shadow. You are a mighty man of valor. You are a loving husband. You are a responsible father. You are a leader in your community. You are a child of the Most High God. You are, can be, and will be a GOOD MAN!

ABOUT THE AUTHOR

Michael L. Henderson Sr. is a hands-on Pastor, trained Christian Counselor and dynamic Spiritual Mentor. He is the Founder and Senior Pastor of New Beginnings Church in Matthews, North Carolina.

He personally coaches pastors and leaders across the country, and speaks at men's conferences, marriage conferences, leadership conferences and revivals.

He is married to his ministry partner, Twanna Henderson. They have one son, Michael Jr.

For Booking Ministry Engagements and Book Signings:

Email: Bookings@MLHMinistries.com

Or send your ministry request to:

MLH Ministries
c/o 7027 Stillwell Road
Matthews, NC 28105